HOLLY
WOOD
STARS

HOLLY WOOD STARS

Photographs from
The Kobal Collection

FOG CITY PRESS

THE PICTURE DESK LIMITED
Managing Director: Lauretta Dives
Designer: Sally Geeve
Editor: Felicity Green Hill
Text: Louise Stein
Research: Rob Gerlach
Picture Editor: Dave Kent
Picture Research: Phil Moad
Digital Image Production: Harriet Simpson
www.picture-desk.com

FOG CITY PRESS
A Division of Weldon Owen Inc.
Chief Executive Officer: John Owen
President: Terry Newell
Chief Operating Officer: Larry Partington
VP of Finance: Liz Yee
VP International Sales: Stuart Laurence
Sales Manager: Emily Jahn
Consulting Publisher: Rebecca Poole Forée
Jacket Design: Angela Williams
Additional Design: Angela Williams
Production: Chris Hemesath, Teri Bell
Production Coordinator: Libby Temple
Copy Editors: Desne Ahlers, Arin Hailey

HOLLYWOOD STARS
Produced by Weldon Owen Inc.
814 Montgomery Street, San Francisco, CA 94133 USA
Tel: (415) 291-0100 **Fax:** (415) 291-8841
In collaboration with The Picture Desk Limited
2 The Quadrant, 135 Salusbury Road, London,
NW6 6RJ, UK
Tel: 44 (207) 624 3500 **Fax:** 44 (207) 624 3355

Printed in China by Leefung-Asco Printers

A WELDON OWEN PRODUCTION

First printed in 2003
10 9 8 7 6 5 4 3 2 1

Library of Congress Cataloging-in-Publication Data is available

ISBN 1-740895-11-8

www.weldonowen.com

CONTENTS

CONTENTS

What makes a star? Trying to define star quality is like attempting to explain sex appeal, and although it's fair to say that the two are closely related, a true Hollywood great owes lasting success to more than just a beautiful or handsome face or a set of impressive vital statistics. Star quality is elusive, exclusive, and magnetic, a combination of dramatic excellence plus an inner luminosity that shines so brightly that we are transfixed, and fantasy merges with reality.

One thing is for certain, a definitive "Top 100" list is impossible to agree upon, and no doubt this book of one hundred stars will spark an entertaining debate. It is worth remembering that while many of the stars featured here are also deemed to be great actors, not all great actors are necessarily stars.

How to choose just one hundred names from such a wealth of talent? There was no easy answer, and in the end the choice had to start with the very essence of stardom: the face—its power, its beauty, its strong intelligence, its very individuality. These are the faces that speak to us, even when silent. They speak of glamour and excitement, of drama, of slapstick and romance, of the myriad stories of human existence that appear on our movie screens. But they also tell us something about ourselves, about our own aspirations and dreams, fears and anxieties, disappointments and triumphs.

For many Hollywood greats there is always that one magical moment, an image that lingers in our minds long after the credits have rolled. How many thousands—

maybe hundreds of thousands—of young men in the seventies launched themselves onto the disco dancefloor in imitation of Travolta's white-suited, snake-hipped bravura performance in *Saturday Night Fever*? Who can forget Julia Roberts swinging down Rodeo Drive in *Pretty Woman* in her polka-dot dress and matching hat or Brando's *Godfather* in the garden advising the young "don," Michael Corleone (played by Al Pacino), on how to recognize his eventual betrayer?

Back in the early days of Hollywood we, the fans, knew only what the studios wished us to know about our idols and saw only what they thought it was suitable for us to see. These beautifully photographed, carefully posed images of the gods and goddesses of the silver screen imprinted themselves on our minds. Today, with the advent of television, these stars are much more accessible; the revealing close-up has replaced the distant glamour, and there is a gritty reality about our contemporary idols. Our fascination with them, their lives, their careers, their loves, and their personal dramas, however, remains as strong as ever. Star quality today enriches our lives and entertains and fascinates us as it has always done.

Many of the films in which our Hollywood greats gave their all have become classics, watched and rewatched around the world. Take a look at the key film titles listed alongside each Hollywood star and you will discover a treasure trove of more than a thousand great movies—films worth revisiting and others just waiting for you to discover them.

Enjoy!

JULIE ANDREWS

Julie Andrews's career began when, aged twelve, she was widely acclaimed for the purity of her extraordinarily beautiful soprano voice. She was born Julia Elizabeth Wells in Walton-on-Thames, England, on October 1, 1935, and grew up in a show-business family. In 1956 she achieved instant stardom when she created the role of Eliza Doolittle in the Broadway smash hit *My Fair Lady*. Her first film role as Mary Poppins won her the Academy Award as Best Actress. *The Sound of Music*, one of the biggest film successes of all time, came a year later. Andrews has also excelled in nonsinging roles, has made many television appearances, and returned to Broadway in a stage version of her hit film *Victor/Victoria*.

Studio Portrait
(MGM 1964)

The Sound of Music
(20th Century Fox 1965)

KEY FILMS
Mary Poppins, 1964
The Americanization of
   Emily, 1964
The Sound of Music, 1965
Torn Curtain, 1966
Thoroughly Modern Millie,
   1967
Ten, 1979
Victor/Victoria, 1982

Thoroughly Modern Millie
(Universal 1967)

Mary Poppins
(Walt Disney 1964)

"Supercalifragilisticexpialidocious!"

"Working with her is like being hit over the head by a Valentine's card."

CHRISTOPHER PLUMMER

Ten
with Bo Derek and
Dudley Moore
(Orion/Warner Bros 1979)
ph: Bruce McBroom

Torn Curtain
with Paul Newman
(Universal 1966)

FRED ASTAIRE

The greatest popular dancer of the twentieth century was born Frederick Austerlitz on May 10, 1899, in Omaha, Nebraska. He was a major stage star dancing with his sister Adele long before he ever made a film. In his first movie he partnered with Joan Crawford, and in his second, Ginger Rogers, with whom he made ten wildly successful musicals. Song after classic song from major songwriters were introduced in the Astaire/Rogers movies. Astaire's other dance partners included Rita Hayworth, Judy Garland, Cyd Charisse, and Audrey Hepburn. He was given an honorary Academy Award in 1950. He died in 1987.

Studio Portrait
(RKO 1935)
ph: Ernest Bachrach

Funny Face
(Paramount 1957)

KEY FILMS
Top Hat, 1935
Swing Time, 1936
Shall We Dance, 1937
Holiday Inn, 1942
You Were Never Lovelier, 1942
Easter Parade, 1948
The Barkleys of Broadway, 1949
The Band Wagon, 1953
Funny Face, 1957
On the Beach, 1959

Broadway Melody of 1940
with Eleanor Powell
(MGM 1940)

Swing Time
with Ginger Rogers
(RKO 1936)

*"I suppose
I made it look
easy, but gee
whiz, did I
work and worry."*

The Band Wagon
with Cyd Charisse
(MGM 1953)

LAUREN BACALL

The Big Sleep
(Warner Brothers 1946)
ph: Scotty Welbourne

Betty Joan Perske, born September 16, 1924, in New York City, was working as a teenage model when her photograph was spotted in a fashion magazine by the wife of Hollywood director Howard Hawks. Hawks, struck by the young girl's sultry beauty and independent attitude, cast her in *To Have and Have Not* opposite Humphrey Bogart. This partnership made history on and off screen. Bogart and Becall married, had two children, and made three other films together. After Bogart's death, Bacall's career expanded to include several roles on Broadway as well as on the London stage.

Designing Woman
(MGM 1957)
ph: James Manatt

KEY FILMS
To Have and Have Not, 1944
The Big Sleep, 1946
Dark Passage, 1947
Key Largo, 1948
How to Marry a Millionaire, 1953
Written on the Wind, 1956
Designing Woman, 1957
Harper, 1966
The Shootist, 1976
The Mirror Has Two Faces, 1996

Written on the Wind
with Rock Hudson
(Universal 1956)
ph: Ray Jones

How to Marry a Millionaire
with Marilyn Monroe and
Betty Grable
(20th Century Fox 1953)

"*You know
how to whistle,
don't you?
Just put your
lips together
and blow.*"

Studio Portrait
(Warner Brothers 1945)
ph: John Engstead

To Have and Have Not
with Humphrey Bogart
(Warner Brothers 1944)

WARREN BEATTY

The younger brother of actress Shirley MacLaine, Henry Warren Beaty (which he later changed to Beatty) was born on March 10, 1937, in Richmond, Virginia. He became a star with his first film *Splendor in the Grass*, playing opposite Natalie Wood. By 1967, this handsome, intelligent actor had expanded his talents to producing with the runaway success of *Bonnie and Clyde*, in which he also starred. He began co-writing, then directing, and won an Academy Award as Best Director for *Reds*, a film in which he also starred with Diane Keaton and Jack Nicholson. Famous for his many romantic liaisons, he has since married his *Bugsy* co-star Annette Bening and is the father of four children.

Studio Portrait
(1962)

Splendor in the Grass
with Natalie Wood
(Warner Brothers 1961)

KEY FILMS
Splendor in the Grass, 1961
Bonnie and Clyde, 1967
McCabe and Mrs. Miller, 1971
The Parallax View, 1974
Shampoo, 1975
Heaven Can Wait, 1978 (also co-directed)
Reds, 1981 (also directed)
Dick Tracy, 1990 (also directed)
Bugsy, 1991

*"All presidents
want to be
Warren Beatty."*

ALEC BALDWIN

Reds
with Diane Keaton
(Paramount 1981)
ph: David Appleby

Bonnie and Clyde
(Warner Brothers 1967)

Love Affair
with Annette Bening
(Warner Brothers 1994)
ph: David James

McCabe and Mrs. Miller
(Warner Brothers 1971)

INGRID BERGMAN

Ingrid Bergman, who was born in Stockholm, Sweden, on August 19, 1915, wanted to act from childhood. Her first movie role, at age nineteen, made her an instant star in her native land. Four years later David O. Selznick brought her to Hollywood where she won an Academy Award as Best Actress for *Gaslight* in 1944. Her radiance and lack of pretension captivated American audiences who were shocked when, in 1949, she left her husband to live with

Italian director Roberto Rossellini. Marriage to Rossellini brought three children and a career in Europe before her triumphant return to mainstream films with *Anastasia*, which earned her a second Academy Award. She won her third Academy Award as Best Supporting Actress for *Murder on the Orient Express*. Bergman died in London in 1982.

Studio Portrait
(Selznick 1938)
ph: John Engstead

KEY FILMS
Intermezzo, 1939
Dr. Jekyll and Mr. Hyde, 1941
Casablanca, 1942
For Whom the Bell Tolls, 1943
Gaslight, 1944
Spellbound, 1945
Notorious, 1946
Anastasia, 1956
The Inn of the Sixth Happiness, 1958
Murder on the Orient Express, 1974
Autumn Sonata, 1978

Anastasia
(20th Century Fox 1956)

"Here's looking at you, kid."

Joan of Arc
(RKO 1948)
ph: Carlyle Blackwell Jr.

Casablanca
with Humphrey Bogart
(Warner Brothers 1942)

"I didn't choose acting.
It chose me."

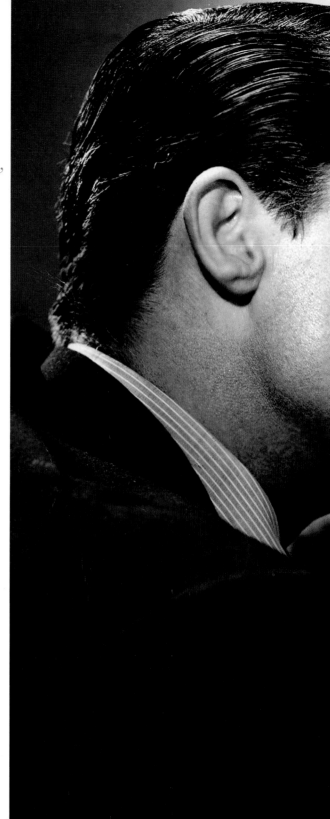

Notorious
with Cary Grant
(RKO 1946)
ph: Ernest Bachrach

HUMPHREY BOGART

"Bogie" was born Humphrey DeForest Bogart in New York City, on December 15, 1899. After serving in the armed forces in World War I, he began his career on the stage. Hollywood noticed him in the Broadway hit *The Petrified Forest* and signed him to repeat the part of the gangster in the screen version. Leading roles followed, but it was starring as the detective Sam Spade in *The Maltese Falcon* in 1941 that made him a movie icon.

His tough-but-vulnerable persona has etched itself on the consciousness of generation after generation. *Casablanca* and the films he made with his fourth wife, Lauren Bacall, remain particular favorites. Bogart won an Academy Award as Best Actor for *The African Queen*. He died in 1957.

High Sierra
(Warner Brothers 1941)
ph: Bert Six

The Caine Mutiny
(Columbia 1954)

KEY FILMS
The Petrified Forest, 1936
Dead End, 1937
High Sierra, 1941
The Maltese Falcon, 1941
Casablanca, 1942
To Have and Have Not, 1944
The Big Sleep, 1946
The Treasure of the Sierra Madre, 1947
Key Largo, 1948
The African Queen, 1951
The Caine Mutiny, 1954

The Maltese Falcon
with Peter Lorre, Mary Astor,
and Sydney Greenstreet
(Warner Brothers 1941)

Casablanca
(Warner Brothers 1942)

Next page
The African Queen
with Katharine Hepburn
(Romulus 1951)

"*There are only a few actors in the world you can have in every scene and not get tired of them. You don't get tired of Bogart.*"

HOWARD HAWKS,
DIRECTOR

Deadline USA
(20th Century Fox 1952)
ph: Frank Powolny

Studio Portrait
(Warner Brothers 1942)
ph: Scotty Welbourne

MARLON BRANDO

Considered by many the greatest screen actor of his generation, Marlon Brando Jr. was born on April 3, 1924, in Omaha, Nebraska, and began his career in the theater. He electrified Broadway with his portrayal of Stanley Kowalski in *A Streetcar Named Desire* and, under the direction of Elia Kazan, re-created the role (and the electricity) in the film version. Three years later he won his first Academy Award as Best Actor for *On the Waterfront*. Brando's unique embodiment of the "Method" acting style illuminated his roles from Shakespeare to musical comedy. He extended his talents to directing and producing as well as starring in *One-Eyed Jacks*. His aging Mafia don in *The Godfather* earned him a second Academy Award. His more recent appearances have been in supporting roles, but his screen charisma remains undiminished.

Studio Portrait
(1951)

Apocalypse Now
(Zoetrope/UA 1979)

KEY FILMS
A Streetcar Named Desire, 1951
Viva Zapata! 1952
Julius Caesar, 1953
The Wild One, 1954
On the Waterfront, 1954
Guys and Dolls, 1955
One-Eyed Jacks, 1961
Mutiny on the Bounty, 1962
The Godfather, 1972
Last Tango in Paris, 1972
Apocalypse Now, 1979

Mutiny on the Bounty
with Trevor Howard
(MGM 1962)
ph: Eric Carpenter

*"Kathie: What are you
rebelling against?
Johnny: What have you got?"*

The Wild One
(Columbia 1954)

A Streetcar Named Desire
with Vivien Leigh
(Warner Brothers 1951)
ph: Bert Six

On the Waterfront
with Eva Marie Saint
(Columbia 1954)

*"I'm gonna make him
an offer he can't refuse."*

The Godfather
(Paramount 1972)

JEFF BRIDGES

Jeffrey Leon Bridges was born on December 4, 1949, in Los Angeles, and made his movie debut a few months later, playing Jane Greer's baby. Son of actor Lloyd Bridges and younger brother of Beau, Jeff entered the family business while still in his teens and made his first big splash in Peter Bogdanovich's film *The Last Picture Show*. This brought him the first of his four Academy Award nominations. Invariably praised by the critics for his superb acting, Bridges's film choices have always centered on meaty roles rather than showy star turns.

The Last Picture Show
with Cybill Shepherd
(Columbia 1971)

Nadine
(Tri-Star 1987)
ph: Ron Phillips

KEY FILMS
The Last Picture Show, 1971
Fat City, 1972
Thunderbolt and Lightfoot, 1974
Starman, 1984
Jagged Edge, 1985
Tucker: The Man and His Dream, 1988
The Fabulous Baker Boys, 1989
The Fisher King, 1991
The Big Lebowski, 1998
The Contender, 2000

Jagged Edge
with Glenn Close
(Columbia 1985)
ph: Elliott Marks

"I don't think I ever went down that movie star path. I always enjoy taking a 90-degree turn from the last thing I did."

The Big Lebowski
(Polygram 1998)
ph: Merrick Morton

SANDRA BULLOCK

S andra Annette Bullock was born in Arlington, Virginia, on July 26, 1964. The daughter of a German opera singer and a voice teacher, she spent much of her formative years living in Germany and Austria. She studied acting in New York with television roles leading to a movie career, and she soared to stardom in *Speed*. Her screen image as the "girl next door" with just a hint of mischief has made her one of Hollywood's highest paid and most popular actresses. Bullock is also active in her own production company.

A Time to Kill
(*Warner Brothers 1996*)
ph: Christine Loss

Speed
with Keanu Reeves
(*20th Century Fox 1994*)
ph: Richard Foreman

KEY FILMS
Wrestling Ernest
    Hemingway, 1992
Speed, 1994
The Net, 1995
While You Were Sleeping,
    1995
A Time to Kill, 1996
Hope Floats, 1998
Divine Secrets of the Ya-Ya
    Sisterhood, 2002
Two Weeks Notice, 2002

**Divine Secrets of the Ya-Ya
Sisterhood**
with Ellen Burstyn
*(Gaylord Films/All Girl
Productions 2002)*
ph: Michael Tackett

In Love and War
(New Line 1996)
ph: Alex Bailey

"I'd rather take risks than make something that's cookie cutter."

RICHARD BURTON

The son of a coal miner, Richard Walter Jenkins, who was born November 10, 1925, in Pontrhydfen, South Wales, took his stage name from the teacher who had guided him to a scholarship to Oxford University. A handsome man with a beautiful speaking voice, Burton's early career included London stage appearances and British movies, followed by several Hollywood films. But superstardom came with his role as Mark Antony in *Cleopatra*, and the torrid romance that developed with his leading lady, Elizabeth Taylor. Their married life made continual headlines and even after

Studio Portrait
(Warner Brothers 1959)
ph: Bert Six

their re-marriage and divorce, they appeared together on the Broadway stage. Burton died in 1984 after completing his role in the film *1984*, based on George Orwell's famous book.

Who's Afraid of Virginia Woolf?
with Elizabeth Taylor
(Warner Brothers 1966)

KEY FILMS
My Cousin Rachel, 1952
The Robe, 1953
Look Back in Anger, 1959
Cleopatra, 1963
The V.I.P.s, 1963
The Night of the Iguana, 1964
The Spy Who Came in from the Cold, 1965
Who's Afraid of Virginia Woolf? 1966
Where Eagles Dare, 1968
1984, 1984

Where Eagles Dare
(MGM 1968)

The Robe
(20th Century Fox 1953)

NICOLAS CAGE

Nicolas Kim Coppola, nephew of the director Francis Ford Coppola, was born on January 7, 1964, in Long Beach, California. Not wishing to capitalize on that connection, he changed his family name and based it on a favorite comic character. His early roles were small, but his strong screen presence began to make an impact, especially in offbeat films such as *Raising Arizona* and *Wild at Heart*. Cage's harrowing performance as a suicidal alcoholic in *Leaving Las Vegas* won him the Academy Award for Best Actor. He directed his first film, *Sonny*, in 2002.

Windtalkers
(MGM 2002)
ph: Stephen Vaughan

City of Angels
(Warner Bros 1998)
ph: Murray Close

KEY FILMS
Birdy, 1984
Peggy Sue Got Married, 1986
Raising Arizona, 1987
Moonstruck, 1987
Wild at Heart, 1990
Honeymoon in Vegas, 1992
Leaving Las Vegas, 1995
Con Air, 1997
Face/Off, 1997
Windtalkers, 2002
Adaptation, 2002

Raising Arizona
(20th Century Fox 1987)
ph: Melinda Sue Gordon

"Hollywood didn't know if I was an
actor or a nut or if I was this crazy character
I was playing. I had developed an image of being
a little bit unusual, different and wild."

Wild at Heart
with Laura Dern
(Propaganda/Polygram 1990)
ph: Stephen Vaughan

JAMES CAGNEY

James Francis Cagney Jr. was born on July 17, 1899, in Manhattan, and grew up on the tough streets of the Yorkville neighborhood. Before he was twenty, he was cast in his first stage show—in "drag"—and quickly learned to sing and dance with flair, appearing in musicals and plays throughout the twenties. Brought to Hollywood by Jack Warner, Cagney became a star with his fourth movie, *The Public Enemy*, and remained a dominant force in films for the rest of his life. He won an Academy Award as Best Actor for *Yankee Doodle Dandy*, in which he played the great American showman and songwriter, George M. Cohan. Cagney died in 1986.

Studio Portrait
(Warner Brothers 1942)
ph: Scotty Welbourne

Yankee Doodle Dandy
(Warner Brothers 1942)

KEY FILMS
The Public Enemy, 1931
Footlight Parade, 1933
A Midsummer Night's
  Dream, 1935
Angels with Dirty Faces,
  1938
The Roaring Twenties, 1939
The Strawberry Blonde,
  1941
Yankee Doodle Dandy, 1942
White Heat, 1949
Love Me or Leave Me, 1955
Ragtime, 1981

Captains of the Clouds
(Warner Brothers 1942)
ph: Scotty Welbourne

The Public Enemy
(Warner Brothers 1931)

Ragtime
(Paramount 1981)

White Heat
(Warner Brothers 1949)

*"One of the biggest actors in the whole
history of the screen. Force, style, truth, and
control — he had everything."*

ORSON WELLES

JIM CARREY

James Eugene Carrey, born January 17, 1962, in Newmarket, Ontario, Canada, knew from an early age that he wanted to perform. He had a difficult adolescence, and when his family suffered a fall in their fortunes, he eventually dropped out of high school. He started working in comedy clubs, learning his craft. Television appearances and small film roles preceded his breakthrough success in *Ace Ventura, Pet Detective*, followed by the megahit, *The Mask*. His brand of manic comedy proved to be box office magic, but he

The Majestic
(Castle Rock 2001)
ph: Ralph Nelson Jr.

also has tried his hand at more serious fare, such as Peter Weir's quirky study of the ultimate reality TV program, *The Truman Show*.

Man on the Moon
with Courtney Love
(Universal 1999)
ph: Francois Duhamel

KEY FILMS
Ace Ventura, Pet Detective, 1994
The Mask, 1994
Dumb & Dumber, 1994
The Truman Show, 1998
Man on the Moon, 1999
Me, Myself & Irene, 2000
The Grinch, 2000

The Truman Show
(Paramount 1998)
ph: Melinda Sue Gordon

"Jim is like a wicked, naughty boy in a man's body.
He has a very real electricity that could crack glass."

PETER WEIR

The Mask
(New Line 1994)
ph: Blake Little

Dumb & Dumber
with Jeff Daniels
(New Line 1994)
ph: Mark Fellman

**Ace Ventura: When
Nature Calls**
(Morgan Creek 1995)
ph: Marsha Blackburn

GEORGE CLOONEY

One Fine Day
(20th Century Fox 1996)
ph: Myles Aronowitzon

George Timothy Clooney, nephew of the famed popular singer Rosemary Clooney, was born in Lexington, Kentucky, on May 6, 1961. Clooney acted in small roles on television for years, but it was in his role as Dr. Doug Ross in the television series *E.R.* that audiences noticed him and he soared to stardom. His saturnine good looks combined with a natural screen presence have made him a major star. His range includes both the commercial and the unusual, such as his wacky role in the Coen brothers' film *O Brother, Where Art Thou?* In recent years Clooney has become involved in producing movies.

Ocean's Eleven
(Warner Brothers 2001)
ph: Bob Marshak

KEY FILMS
One Fine Day, 1996
Out of Sight, 1998
The Thin Red Line, 1998
Three Kings, 1999
O Brother, Where Art Thou?
  2000
The Perfect Storm, 2000
Ocean's Eleven, 2001
Confessions of a Dangerous
  Mind, 2002

Three Kings
with Ice Cube
(Warner Brothers 1999)
ph: Murray Close

Batman and Robin
(Warner Bros/DC Comics
1997)

"George has set a really wonderful example of not becoming a jerk movie star."

ANTHONY EDWARDS

O Brother, Where Art Thou?
with John Turturro and Tim Blake Nelson
(Touchstone 2000)
ph: Melinda Sue Gordon

Out of Sight
(Universal 1998)
ph: Merrick Morton

SEAN CONNERY

For many years, to the movie-going public, Sean Connery was James Bond. The handsome Scots actor, born Thomas Sean Connery in Edinburgh on August 25, 1930, had worked hard on his way to the top, taking dead-end jobs until he drifted into acting. Stage roles and several British films preceded *Dr. No*, the first Bond film, which catapulted him to worldwide stardom. Although he played Bond in another five films, Connery has also appeared in a wide range of roles and won an Academy Award as Best Supporting Actor for *The Untouchables*. Off screen, he is known as a serious golfer. He was knighted by Queen Elizabeth in 1999.

Studio Portrait
(United Artists 1963)

The Untouchables
(Paramount 1987)
ph: Zade Rosenthal

KEY FILMS
Dr. No, 1962
From Russia with Love, 1963
Marnie, 1964
Goldfinger, 1964
The Hill, 1965
The Anderson Tapes, 1971
The Man Who Would Be King, 1975
The Untouchables, 1987
Indiana Jones and the Last Crusade, 1989
Entrapment, 1999

From Russia with Love
with Daniela Bianchi
(EON/UA 1963)

"I'm an actor—it's not brain surgery.
If I do my job right, people won't ask
for their money back."

**The Man Who Would
Be King**
with Michael Caine
(Allied Artists 1975)

**Indiana Jones and
the Last Crusade**
(LucasFilm/Paramount 1989)
ph: Murray Close

GARY COOPER

"Coop" was born Frank James Cooper in Helena, Montana, on May 17, 1901. He was educated for seven years in England and learned to ride a horse on his father's Montana ranch. Settling in Los Angeles, he drifted into silent films, gaining attention for a small role in the classic film *Wings* (1927). His rise to stardom was swift. The epitome of the strong silent type, Cooper became one of the true film greats, a superstar whose career covered more than thirty years. He won two Academy Awards for Best Actor, for *Sergeant York* and *High Noon*. He died in 1961.

Studio Portrait
(Paramount 1934)
ph: C. S. Bull

Sergeant York
(Warner Brothers 1941)
ph: Mac Julian

KEY FILMS
The Virginian, 1929
Morocco, 1930
A Farewell to Arms, 1932
The Lives of a Bengal
    Lancer, 1935
Mr. Deeds Goes to Town,
    1936
Beau Geste, 1939
Meet John Doe, 1941
Sergeant York, 1941
For Whom the Bell Tolls,
    1943
The Fountainhead, 1949
High Noon, 1952
Love in the Afternoon, 1956

*"The fellow is the
world's greatest actor.
He can do with no effort
what the rest of us
spent years trying to learn:
to be perfectly natural."*

JOHN BARRYMORE, ACTOR

Morocco
with Marlene Dietrich
(Paramount 1930)

**The Lives of a
Bengal Lancer**
(Paramount 1935)

Mr. Deeds Goes to Town
with Jean Arthur
(Columbia 1936)

Ball of Fire
with Barbara Stanwyck
(RKO/Samuel Goldwyn 1941)
ph: Robert Coburn

High Noon
(Stanley Kramer/UA 1952)

KEVIN COSTNER

Kevin Michael Costner was born on January 18, 1955, in Lynwood, California. His acting career began with several small roles before getting what should have been his big break in the runaway hit, *The Big Chill*. Unfortunately, his part in that film ended up on the cutting room floor. Playing Eliot Ness in *The Untouchables* finally made him a star, his boyish good looks and quiet presence winning him a large female following. Through his own production company he directed and starred in *Dances with Wolves*, which portrayed the Native American in a sympathetic light. This film won him Academy Awards for both Best Director and Best Picture.

Message in a Bottle
(Warner Brothers 1999)
ph: Ben Glass

Dances with Wolves
(Orion 1990)
ph: Ben Glass

KEY FILMS
Silverado, 1985
No Way Out, 1987
The Untouchables, 1987
Bull Durham, 1988
Field of Dreams, 1989
Dances with Wolves, 1990
  (also directed)
JFK, 1991
The Bodyguard, 1992
Thirteen Days, 2000

"If you say what you mean in this town, you're an outlaw."

The Untouchables
(Paramount 1987)
ph: Zade Rosenthal

No Way Out
(Orion 1987)
ph: S. Karin Epstein

JOAN CRAWFORD

Joan Crawford, the consummate screen star, began life as Lucille Fay Le Sueur, on March 23, 1904, in San Antonio, Texas. Winning a Charleston contest brought her to a Broadway chorus line and then an MGM contract. Through the decades, Crawford honed her screen persona intelligently, progressing from 1920s flappers to 1950s melodramatic heroines, finally winning an Academy Award as Best Actress for *Mildred Pierce*. Late in her career, Crawford had the unexpected success of *What Ever Happened to Baby Jane?* She also entered the business world as executive of her fourth husband's beverage company. She died in 1977.

Studio Portrait
(MGM 1933)
ph: George Hurrell

Mildred Pierce
(Warner Brothers 1945)

KEY FILMS
Our Dancing Daughters, 1928
Grand Hotel, 1932
Rain, 1932
Dancing Lady, 1933
The Gorgeous Hussy, 1936
The Women, 1939
Mildred Pierce, 1945
Harriet Craig, 1950
Sudden Fear, 1952
Johnny Guitar, 1954
What Ever Happened to Baby Jane? 1962

"If I can't be me, I don't want to be anybody. I was born that way."

Sally, Irene and Mary
with Constance Bennett
and Sally O'Neil
(MGM 1925)

Dancing Lady
with Clark Gable
(MGM 1933)
ph: George Hurrell

The Women
with Norma Shearer and
Rosalind Russell
(MGM 1939)
ph: Laszlo Willinger

Letty Lynton
(MGM 1932)
ph: George Hurrell

RUSSELL CROWE

Russell Ira Crowe was born on April 7, 1964, in Wellington, New Zealand. He left school early to try his hand at acting and music, moving to Australia, where he worked steadily on the stage. His first film role came in 1990. A succession of Australian films followed as well as several film awards. He first made a splash on the American screen in *L.A. Confidential*. Two years later, his role in *The Insider* brought him an Academy Award nomination, and the following year he won Best Actor for *Gladiator*. Despite his tough exterior, he has been praised by the critics as a thoughtful and highly intelligent actor who immerses himself in his roles, which his most recently nominated performance in *A Beautiful Mind* makes abundantly clear.

L.A. Confidential
(Monarchy/Regency 1997)
ph: Peter Sorel

Romper Stomper
(Seon Films 1992)
ph: Peter Leiss

KEY FILMS
Romper Stomper, 1992
L.A. Confidential, 1997
The Insider, 1999
Gladiator, 2000
Proof of Life, 2000
A Beautiful Mind, 2001

*"There's a fire in him that burns
all night long, all day long, all the time."*

BURT REYNOLDS

Proof of Life
with Meg Ryan
(Bel Air/Castle Rock 2000)
ph: Ralph Nelson Jr.

A Beautiful Mind
(Dreamworks/Universal 2001)
ph: Eli Reed

Gladiator
(Dreamworks/Universal 2000)
ph: Jaap Buitendijk

TOM CRUISE

Thomas Cruise Mapother IV was born on July 3, 1962, in Syracuse, New York. Raised in genteel poverty by his mother, he seriously considered becoming a monk, but a part in a high school production soon changed his mind. His big Hollywood breakthrough came with *Top Gun*, a high-grossing success, but his roles in *Rain Man* and *Born on the Fourth of July* proved that he had talent as well as startling good looks. He has been nominated for Academy Awards three times and recently became involved in film production.

Vanilla Sky
(Cruise-Wagner 2001)
ph: Neal Preston

Born on the Fourth of July
(Universal 1989)
ph: Roland Neveu

KEY FILMS
Top Gun, 1986
The Color of Money, 1986
Rain Man, 1988
Born on the Fourth of July, 1989
Mission: Impossible, 1996
Jerry Maguire, 1996
Eyes Wide Shut, 1999
Magnolia, 1999
Mission: Impossible II, 2000
Minority Report, 2002

Mission: Impossible
(Paramount 1996)
ph: Murray Close

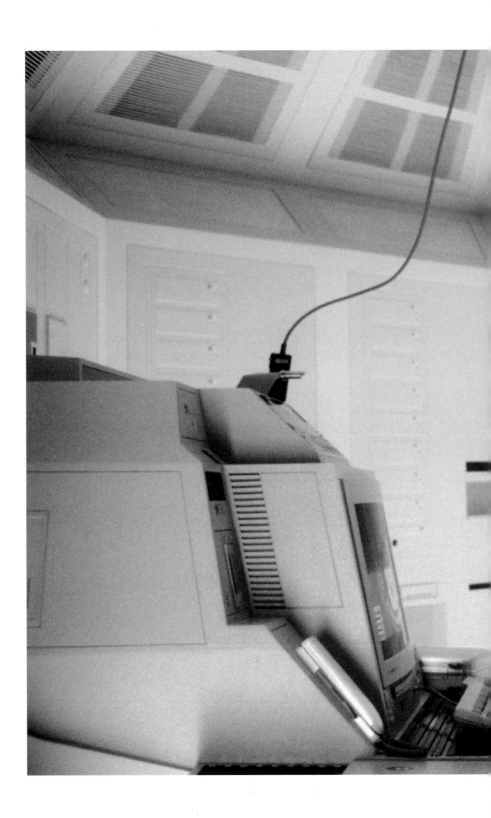

Rain Man
with Dustin Hoffman
(United Artists 1988)
ph: Stephen Vaughan

Top Gun
(Paramount 1986)
ph: Ralph Nelson Jr.

"*On screen the camera adores him so much that there's a risk that he may come out looking even more gorgeous than his leading lady.*"

BOB CORT, PRODUCER

Minority Report
with Samantha Morton
(20th Century Fox/
Dreamworks 2002)
ph: David James

Jerry Maguire
(Columbia 1996)
ph: Andrew Cooper

TONY CURTIS

orn Bernard Schwartz on June 3, 1925, in the Bronx, New York, Curtis grew up as a street kid on the East Side of Manhattan. After a stint in the Navy he was discovered by a Universal talent scout and put under contract by the studio. He was groomed for stardom as a romantic leading man, and his matinee-idol good looks brought him hordes of female fans. He soon surprised audiences with his versatility, giving strong dramatic performances in films with Burt Lancaster and Sidney Poitier as well as showing a wonderful comic ability in Billy Wilder's classic, *Some Like It Hot*. Curtis had an eleven-year marriage to MGM star Janet Leigh, and actress Jamie Lee Curtis is one of their daughters.

Studio Portrait
(Paramount 1960)

The Boston Strangler
(20th Century Fox 1968)

KEY FILMS
City Across the River, 1949
The Prince Who Was a
    Thief, 1951
Trapeze, 1956
Sweet Smell of Success, 1957
The Defiant Ones, 1958
Some Like It Hot, 1959
Operation Petticoat, 1959
Spartacus, 1960
The Boston Strangler, 1968
The Last Tycoon, 1976

*"Hollywood . . .
the most
sensational
merry-go-round
ever built."*

The Sweet Smell of Success
(United Artists 1957)

Some Like It Hot
with Marilyn Monroe
(United Artists 1959)

BETTE DAVIS

For Ruth Elizabeth Davis, born April 5, 1908, in Lowell, Massachusetts, the climb to the top began with stage appearances and then inferior films that hardly gave her room to display her considerable dramatic talents. Her first Academy Award, for *Dangerous*, and continuous battles with her studio, Warner Brothers, eventually resulted in her being given first-class parts in first-class films. She excelled playing strong-willed women, as in her second Academy Award–winning performance in *Jezebel* and her memorable

Whatever Happened to Baby Jane?
(Warner Brothers 1962)

portrayal of Margo Channing in *All About Eve*. All told, she received nine Academy Award nominations. A demanding and exacting perfectionist, Davis continued working almost until her death at the age of 81, in 1989.

Studio Portrait
(Warner Brothers 1932)
ph: Elmer Fryer

KEY FILMS:
Of Human Bondage, 1934
Dangerous, 1935
Jezebel, 1938
The Private Lives of
    Elizabeth and Essex, 1939
The Letter, 1940
The Little Foxes, 1941
Now Voyager, 1942
All About Eve, 1950
What Ever Happened to
    Baby Jane? 1962
The Whales of August, 1988

Now Voyager
with Paul Henreid
(Warner Brothers 1942)

Jezebel
with Henry Fonda
(Warner Brothers 1938)

"If Hollywood didn't work out, I was prepared to be the best secretary in the world."

▸ Next page
The Letter
(Warner Brothers 1940)

DORIS DAY

Born Doris Mary Ann Kappelhoff on April 3, 1924, in Cincinnati, Ohio, Doris Day had her first success as a big-band singer. Her rendition of the song "Sentimental Journey" was a major hit during the days of World War II, and post-war Hollywood beckoned the blonde, perky singer. Almost overnight, Day hit movie stardom, charming the public in a series of musicals. By the 1950s she was rated the top female star in the United States, proving equally adept at comedy and drama. In an Academy Award–nominated performance, she traded wisecracks with Rock Hudson in *Pillow Talk*, one of Hollywood's most successful comedies. Her gritty depiction of the real life song-and-dance girl in *Love Me or Leave Me* won plaudits from her co-star, James Cagney. She also appeared in her own television series.

Studio Portrait
(MGM 1956)

Calamity Jane
(Warner Brothers 1953)

KEY FILMS
Romance on the High Seas, 1948
On Moonlight Bay, 1951
Calamity Jane, 1953
Young at Heart, 1955
Love Me or Leave Me, 1955
The Man Who Knew Too Much, 1956
The Pajama Game, 1957
Pillow Talk, 1959
Midnight Lane, 1960
That Touch of Mink, 1962

The Pajama Game
with John Raitt
(Warner Brothers 1957)

Love Me or Leave Me
(MGM 1955)

"Learning a part was like acting out the lyrics of a song."

Pillow Talk
with Rock Hudson
(Universal 1959)

ROBERT DE NIRO

Robert De Niro was born on August 17, 1943, in New York City. Acting since his teens, he attracted attention in the independent low-budget film *Mean Streets*, directed by Martin Scorsese, with whom De Niro has since forged an enduring creative partnership. Cast in *The Godfather, Part II*, as the young version of Brando's don, De Niro won an Academy Award for Best Supporting Actor for his imaginative portrayal. As Scorsese's unbalanced

The Godfather, Part II
(Paramount 1974)

Taxi Driver, he seemed to epitomize the troubled 1970s, and in another Scorsese film, *Raging Bull*, De Niro played the boxer Jake La Motta, a role that earned him an Academy Award for Best Actor. Considered one of the finest actors of his generation, De Niro is famed for immersing himself completely in his roles.

GoodFellas
(Warner Brothers 1990)
ph: Barry Wetcher

KEY FILMS:
Mean Streets, 1974
The Godfather, Part II, 1974
Taxi Driver, 1976
The Deer Hunter, 1978
Raging Bull, 1980
Once upon a Time in
   America, 1983
GoodFellas, 1990
Cape Fear, 1991
Heat, 1995
Casino, 1995
Analyze This, 1999
Meet the Parents, 2000

Taxi Driver
(Columbia 1976)

Raging Bull
(United Artists 1980)
ph: Brian Hamill

New York, New York
with Liza Minelli
(United Artists 1977)
ph: Bruce McBroom

Meet the Parents
(Universal/Dreamworks 2000)

"He finds release and fulfillment in becoming other people."

ELIA KAZAN, DIRECTOR

JAMES DEAN

Studio Portrait
(Warner Brothers 1955)
ph: Floyd McCarty

Cult icon James Dean was born James Byron Dean in Marion, Indiana, on February 9, 1931. As a young actor in New York, Dean received critical acclaim for his performances on stage and television, and he headed west to make his way in films. Elia Kazan cast him as the lead in *East of Eden*, but his second film, *Rebel Without a Cause*, hit the movie theaters first, and the young rebel he played struck an extraordinarily deep chord

with the world's teenagers. Although Dean had only three films to his credit before his untimely death in an auto accident on September 30, 1955, he is still considered a major movie star. He was nominated twice for an Academy Award as Best Actor.

Studio Portrait
(Warner Brothers 1955)
ph: Bert Six

KEY FILMS
East of Eden, 1955
Rebel Without a Cause,
   1955
Giant, 1956

Rebel Without a Cause
with Natalie Wood
(Warner Brothers 1955)
ph: Floyd McCarty

"James Dean was the strongest
influence on any actor that ever stepped
in front of the camera."

MARTIN SHEEN

East of Eden
(Warner Brothers 1955)

Next page
Giant
(Warner Brothers 1956)

JOHNNY DEPP

John Christopher Depp III was born in Owensboro, Kentucky, on June 9, 1963, and grew up in Florida. A high school dropout who was more interested in music and acting than in academia, Depp made his way to Los Angeles where he was cast in small film roles. His big break came when he landed the lead in the TV series *21 Jump Street*. Overnight, he became a star and a teen heartthrob. In his film career, he has chosen interesting, often offbeat projects, such as the films he has made with maverick director Tim Burton, including *Ed Wood* and *Sleepy Hollow*. Depp also makes more commercial movies such as *Donnie Brasco*, where he more than acquitted himself playing opposite the legendary Al Pacino.

Cry-Baby
(Universal 1990)
ph: Greg Gorman

Ed Wood
(Touchstone 1994)
ph: Suzanne Tenner

KEY FILMS
Cry-Baby, 1990
Edward Scissorhands, 1990
Benny & Joon, 1993
What's Eating Gilbert Grape, 1993
Ed Wood, 1994
Don Juan DeMarco, 1995
Donnie Brasco, 1997
Fear and Loathing in Las Vegas, 1998
Sleepy Hollow, 1999
Chocolat, 2000
Blow, 2001

"The characters I've played, that I've responded to, there has been a lost-soul quality to them."

Fear and Loathing in Las Vegas
with Benicio Del Toro
(Universal 1998)
ph: Peter Mountain

Edward Scissorhands
(20th Century Fox 1990)
ph: Zade Rosenthal

CAMERON DIAZ

I t's amazing to think that Cameron Diaz, who was born on August 30, 1972, in San Diego, California, was a tomboy while she was growing up. But at sixteen, her beauty earned her a contract with the famous Elle modeling agency, and she worked steadily and successfully as a model until, at age twenty-one, she asked

to audition for *The Mask*, starring Jim Carrey. She was astonished to find herself chosen to play the lead in what became a big hit. Since then, her movie roles have been varied, from low-budget films to the big box-office hit, *There's Something About Mary*, whose co-director, Bobby Farrelly, praised her lack of ego, calling her "one of the guys."

Studio Portrait
(Columbia 2000)
ph: Darren Michaels

There's Something About Mary
(20th Century Fox 1998)
ph: Glenn Watson

KEY FILMS
The Mask, 1994
My Best Friend's Wedding, 1997
There's Something About Mary, 1998
Being John Malkovich, 1999
Charlie's Angels, 2000
Vanilla Sky, 2001
Gangs of New York, 2002

"Your regrets aren't what you did, but what you didn't do. So I take every opportunity."

A Life Less Ordinary
(Polygram 1997)
ph: Darren Michaels

Charlie's Angels
with Drew Barrymore
and Lucy Lui
(Columbia 2000)
ph: Darren Michaels

LEONARDO DiCAPRIO

Leonardo Wilhelm DiCaprio's birth on November 11, 1974, in Los Angeles, followed the divorce of his parents. He left school at sixteen and was cast in a television series, which led to small film parts. But it was his astonishing performance in *What's Eating Gilbert Grape* that brought him critical acclaim and an Academy Award nomination. His performance as Romeo in *William Shakespeare's Romeo and Juliet* appealed to his own generation, as much for his angelic good looks as for his ability to speak Shakespeare's poetry. DiCaprio's super-stardom status was assured with the release of *Titanic*, the highest-grossing film made to date.

The Beach
(20th Century Fox 2000)
ph: Peter Mountain

What's Eating Gilbert Grape
with Juliette Lewis and
Johnny Depp
(Paramount 1993)
ph: Peter Iovino

KEY FILMS
This Boy's Life, 1993
What's Eating Gilbert Grape,
   1993
The Basketball Diaries,
   1995
William Shakespeare's
   Romeo and Juliet,
   1996
Titanic, 1997
The Beach, 2000
Gangs of New York, 2002

*"You can either be a vain movie star,
or you can try to shed some light on different
aspects of the human condition."*

Titanic
with Kate Winslet
*(20th Century
Fox/Paramount 1997)
ph: Merie W. Wallace*

MARLENE DIETRICH

Born Maria Magdalena Dietrich on December 27, 1901, in Berlin, Dietrich was well known both on the German stage and in films before making the movie that electrified the world, *The Blue Angel*, directed by Josef von Sternberg. Paramount Pictures brought her to Hollywood as their answer to MGM's Garbo, and along with her came von Sternberg, with whom she made six more films. Dietrich quickly learned the intricacies of filmmaking, using this knowledge with skill to preserve her screen mystique. For her unceasing work for the Allied cause during World War II, France awarded her the Legion of Honor. When film work slowed, Dietrich, at that time the most glamorous of grandmothers, played clubs and theaters around the world, singing the songs she had made famous. She died a recluse in Paris in 1992.

Studio Portrait
(Paramount 1934)
ph: William Walling Jr.

The Devil Is a Woman
(Paramount 1935)
ph: E.R. Richee

KEY FILMS
The Blue Angel, 1929
Morocco, 1930
Shanghai Express, 1932
Desire, 1936
Destry Rides Again, 1939
A Foreign Affair, 1948
Stage Fright, 1950
Witness for the Prosecution, 1957
Touch of Evil, 1958
Judgment at Nuremberg, 1961

*"If she had nothing but her voice, she could break
your heart with it. But she also had that beautiful body
and the timeless loveliness of her face."*

ERNEST HEMINGWAY

Destry Rides Again
with James Stewart
(Universal 1939)
ph: Sherman Clark

Morocco
(Paramount 1930)
ph: E. R. Richee

Dishonored
(Paramount 1931)

Blonde Venus
with Cary Grant
(Paramount 1932)
ph: Don English

Next page
Shanghai Express
with Clive Brook
(Paramount 1932)
ph: Don English

KIRK DOUGLAS

The life of Kirk Douglas, who was born Issur Danielovitch Demsky on December 9, 1916, in Amsterdam, New York, is a rags to riches story. Son of a poor immigrant family, he made his escape from childhood poverty via the stage and subsequent service in the Navy. After World War II he returned to the stage, then moved on to Hollywood where his film career skyrocketed with *Champion,* in which he first displayed the passion and energy that are the hallmarks of his screen persona. Nominated twice for Academy Awards, this dynamic actor has made many distinguished films, directed two, and produced a number through his own production company.

Studio Portrait
(Paramount 1946)
ph: A. L. "Whitey" Schafer

Champion
with Marilyn Maxwell
(United Artists 1949)

KEY FILMS
A Letter to Three Wives, 1949
Champion, 1949
Ace in the Hole, 1951
Detective Story, 1951
The Bad and the Beautiful, 1952
Lust for Life, 1956
Gunfight at the O.K. Corral, 1957
Paths of Glory, 1957
The Vikings, 1958
Spartacus, 1960 (also co-produced)
Lonely Are the Brave, 1962
Posse, 1975 (also directed)

The Bad and the Beautiful
with Barry Sullivan
(MGM 1952)

Spartacus
(Bryna/Universal 1960)

"I think half the success in life comes from first finding out what you really want to do. And then going ahead and doing it."

The Vikings
(Bryna/UA 1958)

Lust for Life
(MGM 1956)

MICHAEL DOUGLAS

Michael Kirk Douglas, the eldest son of Kirk Douglas, was born in New Brunswick, New Jersey, on September 25, 1944. Douglas had made a few minor films and appeared in the TV series *The Streets of San Francisco* before he triumphed in his first bid as producer with *One Flew over the Cuckoo's Nest*, which won the Academy Award for Best Picture. Douglas then broke through to major stardom with *Romancing the Stone*, and he won an Academy Award for Best Actor for his performance as an amoral stockbroker in *Wall Street*. His talent as both an actor and a producer has resulted in a number of highly acclaimed, commercially successful films.

Wall Street
(20th Century Fox 1987)
ph: Andy Schwartz

Falling Down
(Warner Brothers 1993)
ph: Arnold Kopelson

KEY FILMS
The China Syndrome, 1979
 (also producer)
Romancing the Stone, 1984
 (also producer)
Jewel of the Nile, 1985
 (also producer)
Fatal Attraction, 1987
Wall Street, 1987
The War of the Roses, 1989
Basic Instinct, 1992
Falling Down, 1993
Wonder Boys, 2000
Traffic, 2000
One Night at McCool's, 2001
 (also producer)

*"Acting is
tunnel vision,
producing
360-degree
vision."*

Romancing the Stone
with Kathleen Turner
*(20th Century Fox 1984)
ph: Chas Gerretsen-Mega*

Fatal Attraction
with Glenn Close
*(Paramount 1987)
ph: Andy Schwartz*

One Night at McCool's
(Further Films 2001)
ph: Jamie Midgley

Wonder Boys
(Paramount 2000)
ph: Frank Conner

FAYE DUNAWAY

Dorothy Faye Dunaway was born in Bascom, Florida, on January 4, 1941. After college she played leading roles on Broadway and made her film debut in *The Happening* (1967). However, it was another film released that same year that catapulted her to fame: *Bonnie and Clyde*. Her "look" in that film influenced the fashions of the late 1960s, as did her elegant

Network
(United Artists 1976)
ph: Michael Ginsburg

wardrobe in *The Thomas Crown Affair* the following year. *Bonnie and Clyde* brought her an Academy Award nomination, *Chinatown* another, and she won the Best Actress award for *Network*. Statuesque and imperious, she was a natural to play Joan Crawford in the biopic *Mommie Dearest*, and those qualities are still evident in the character roles she now accepts.

Studio Portrait
(Warner Brothers 1967)

KEY FILMS
Bonnie and Clyde, 1967
The Thomas Crown Affair,
    1968
Little Big Man, 1970
The Three Musketeers, 1973
Chinatown, 1974
Three Days of the Condor,
    1975
Network, 1976
Mommie Dearest, 1981
Barfly, 1987
The Chamber, 1996

"Put simply, she has that twice-as-big quality . . .
she belongs up there with the greats."

PADDY CHAYEVSKY, SCREENWRITER

Chinatown
with Jack Nicholson
(Paramount 1974)

Bonnie and Clyde
(Warner Brothers 1967)

CLINT EASTWOOD

Clinton Eastwood Jr. was born in San Francisco on May 31, 1930. He was among the last fledgling actors to be educated at Universal Studio's talent school. After playing small roles in films, he was cast as the lead in the TV series *Rawhide*, which ran for seven years. The Italian "spaghetti Western," *A Fistful of Dollars*, however, is what made him a star. He has since stamped his laconic qualities on a series of memorable screen characters, including the formidable detective Dirty Harry. Given Eastwood's fine understanding of the art of filmmaking, his taking on the role of director on many of his films was a natural progression, one that culminated in the Academy Awards he won for Best Picture and Best Director for *Unforgiven*.

Studio Portrait
(ca. 1960)
ph: John Engstead

Dirty Harry
(Warner Brothers 1971)
ph: Bernie Abramson

KEY FILMS
A Fistful of Dollars, 1964
Coogan's Bluff, 1968
The Beguiled, 1971
Play Misty for Me, 1971
  (also directed)
Dirty Harry, 1971
Escape from Alcatraz, 1979
Pale Rider, 1985
  (also directed)
Bird, 1988 (only directed)
Unforgiven, 1992
  (also directed)
In the Line of Fire, 1993
The Bridges of Madison
  County, 1995 (also
  directed)

For a Few Dollars More
*(Gonzales/Constantin/PEA
1965)*

Coogan's Bluff
(Universal 1968)

Escape from Alcatraz
(Paramount 1979)
ph: Ron Grover

Every Which Way but Loose
(Warner Brothers 1977)
ph: Gemma La Mana

"I love every aspect of the creation of motion pictures and I guess I am committed to it for life."

Unforgiven
(Warner Brothers 1992)
ph: Murray Close

ERROL FLYNN

Perhaps the most famed of movie swashbucklers, Errol Leslie Thomson Flynn was born on June 20, 1909, in Hobart, Tasmania. As a young man he took many adventurous jobs before landing his first acting role in a British film. Signed to a Hollywood contract, Flynn, with dashing swordsmanship in *Captain Blood*, ignited his box-office appeal. A major star for twenty years, he was as well known for his wild life and womanizing as for his acting abilities, which were in fact considerable. His autobiography, *My Wicked, Wicked Ways*, celebrates those disparate qualities that enhanced his screen image. He died of a heart attack in 1959.

Studio Portrait
(Warner Brothers 1940)
ph: George Hurrell

The Adventures of Robin Hood
(Warner Brothers 1938)

KEY FILMS
Captain Blood, 1935
The Charge of the Light
   Brigade, 1936
The Adventures of Robin
   Hood, 1938
Dodge City, 1939
The Private Lives of
   Elizabeth and Essex, 1939
The Sea Hawk, 1940
They Died with Their Boots
   On, 1941
Objective, Burma! 1945
Kim, 1950
The Sun Also Rises, 1957
Too Much Too Soon, 1958

Dodge City
with Olivia De Havilland
(Warner Brothers 1939)

**They Died with Their
Boots On**
(Warner Brothers 1941)

"The public has always expected me to be a playboy, and a decent chap never lets his public down."

The Charge of the Light Brigade
(Warner Brothers 1936)

The Sea Hawk
(Warner Brothers 1940)
ph: Mac Julian

HENRY FONDA

Henry Jaynes Fonda was born on May 16, 1905, in Grand Island, Nebraska. His early experience performing on the stage was in summer stock with a group of contemporaries including James Stewart, with whom he formed a lifelong friendship. Fonda's success on Broadway led him to Hollywood, and within a few years he was a major star, his screen persona encapsulating the best of the American character. After serving in the Navy during World War II, Fonda returned to Broadway with *Mister Roberts*, a role he also played successfully on screen. A lifetime of distinguished performances garnered him an Honorary Academy Award in 1981. He also won the Best Actor Academy Award for *On Golden Pond*, his last film before his death in 1982.

Studio Portrait
(Paramount 1941)
ph: A. L. "Whitey" Schafer

Mister Roberts
(Warner Brothers 1955)

KEY FILMS
You Only Live Once, 1937
Jesse James, 1939
Young Mr. Lincoln, 1939
The Grapes of Wrath, 1940
The Lady Eve, 1941
My Darling Clementine, 1946
Mister Roberts, 1955
The Wrong Man, 1956
12 Angry Men, 1957
   (also produced)
Once upon a Time in the West, 1969
On Golden Pond, 1981

My Darling Clementine
(20th Century Fox 1946)

*"I ain't really Henry Fonda.
Nobody could have
that much integrity."*

The Grapes of Wrath
(20th Century Fox 1940)

Next page
The Lady Eve
with Barbara Stanwyck
(Paramount 1941)
ph: R. E. Richardson

JANE FONDA

The career of Jane Seymour Fonda, born on December 21, 1937, in New York City, has been an amazing seesaw between Hollywood and France, mainstream work and political activism. Fonda studied art in Paris and did some modeling before her Broadway debut, followed by film appearances. She married French director Roger Vadim and made several films with him in France. After their divorce, she returned to Hollywood. Her brilliant performance in *Klute* won her an Academy Award for Best Actress, as did another serious role in *Coming Home*. She later became a successful businesswoman in the physical fitness industry. She and her father, Henry Fonda, appeared together as father and daughter in *On Golden Pond*.

Studio Portrait
(1968)

Klute
(Warner Brothers 1971)

KEY FILMS
Period of Adjustment, 1962
Cat Ballou, 1965
Barbarella, 1968
They Shoot Horses, Don't
   They? 1969
Klute, 1971
Julia, 1977
Coming Home, 1978
The China Syndrome, 1979
Nine to Five, 1980
On Golden Pond, 1981

"People think actresses find public speaking easy, and it's not easy at all; we're used to hiding behind masks."

Cat Ballou
(Columbia 1965)

Barefoot in the Park
with Robert Redford
(Paramount 1967)

HARRISON FORD

Harrison Ford, born on July 13, 1942, in Chicago, was one of the last contract players in the old studio system during the late 1960s. Small parts led nowhere, and he worked as a carpenter to support his family. Stardom came relatively late but in breathtaking form with his role as Han Solo in *Star Wars*, one of the most successful films ever made. Two *Star Wars* sequels plus the Indiana Jones series have been balanced by interesting artistic choices such as *Blade Runner, Witness, Working Girl,* and *Presumed Innocent*—all demonstrating Ford's wide range as an actor.

Studio Portrait
(Paramount 1981)

What Lies Beneath
with Michelle Pfeiffer
(Dreamworks/Amblin 2000)
ph: Francois Duhamel

KEY FILMS
American Graffiti, 1973
Star Wars, 1977
The Empire Strikes Back, 1980
Raiders of the Lost Ark, 1981
Blade Runner, 1982
Return of the Jedi, 1983
Witness, 1985
Working Girl, 1988
Patriot Games, 1992
The Fugitive, 1993
What Lies Beneath, 2000

Blade Runner
(Ladd Company/WB 1982)
ph: Stephen Vaughan

Working Girl
with Melanie Griffith
and Sigourney Weaver
(20th Century Fox 1988)
ph: Jean Pagliuso

Next page
Star Wars
with Mark Hamill and
Carrie Fisher
*(Lucasfilm/20th Century
Fox 1977)*
ph: John Jay

"I had no expectation of the level of adulation that would come my way. I just wanted to make a living with a regular role in a television series."

Clear and Present Danger
(Paramount 1994)
ph: Bruce McBroom

Indiana Jones and the Last Crusade
(Lucasfilm/Paramount 1989)
ph: Murray Close

JODIE FOSTER

Alicia Christian Foster was born in Los Angeles on November 19, 1962. From babyhood she was appearing in TV commercials, modeling, and eventually acting. As a child star she played both cute Disney heroines and the feisty child prostitute in *Taxi Driver*. Foster took time off from acting to go to college, graduating from Yale magna cum laude. The return to Hollywood by this exceptionally intelligent actress produced two Academy Awards for Best Actress for both *The Accused* and *The Silence of the Lambs*. She has also directed and produced several films.

Studio Portrait
(ca. 1985)

The Accused
(Paramount 1988)
ph: Bruce McBroom

KEY FILMS
Alice Doesn't Live Here
   Anymore, 1974
Taxi Driver, 1976
Bugsy Malone, 1976
Hotel New Hampshire, 1984
The Accused, 1988
The Silence of the Lambs,
   1991
Little Man Tate, 1991
   (also directed)
Contact, 1997
The Panic Room, 2002

Taxi Driver
(Columbia 1976)

The Silence of the Lambs
with Scott Glenn and
Anthony Hopkins
(Orion 1991)
ph: Ken Regan

Contact
(Warner Brothers 1997)
ph: Francois Duhamel

"I'm interested in directing movies about situations that I've lived, so they are almost a personal essay about what I've come to believe in."

The Panic Room
with Kristen Stewart
(Columbia 2002)
ph: Merrick Morton

CLARK GABLE

William Clark Gable was born in Cadiz, Ohio, on February 1, 1901. He was bitten early by the acting bug but worked at many jobs before breaking into the theater. Appearances on Broadway led to an MGM contract, and he was soon one of Hollywood's biggest stars, referred to by critics and public alike as the "King." He was loaned out by MGM to make *It Happened One Night,* which unexpectedly became a huge success, winning Academy Awards both for Best Picture and for Gable as Best Actor. When *Gone with the Wind* was to be filmed, there could be no other choice of actor to play Rhett Butler. After the tragic death of his wife, Carole Lombard, in an airplane accident, he served in the Army Air Corps during World War II, returning to filmmaking in 1945. He died soon after completing *The Misfits,* which was also Marilyn Monroe's last film.

Studio Portrait
(1947)
ph: John Engstead

It Happened One Night
with Claudette Colbert
(Columbia 1934)

KEY FILMS
Red Dust, 1932
It Happened One Night,
    1934
Mutiny on the Bounty, 1935
Call of the Wild, 1935
San Francisco, 1936
Gone with the Wind, 1939
Command Decision, 1948
Mogambo, 1953
Teacher's Pet, 1958
The Misfits, 1961

Gone with the Wind
with Vivien Leigh
(Selznick/MGM 1939)

The Misfits
with Marilyn Monroe
(UA/Seven Arts 1961)

No Man of Her Own
with Carole Lombard
(Paramount 1932)
ph: Otto Dyar

*"I'm just a lucky slob who happened to be
in the right place at the right time."*

Call of the Wild
with Loretta Young
(20th Century Fox/UA 1935)

Mutiny on the Bounty
(MGM 1935)

GRETA GARBO

Greta Louisa Gustafsson, born in Stockholm on September 16, 1905, was working as a salesgirl when she won a scholarship to drama school. Her first film, *Gösta Berling's Saga*, was a big hit in Europe and led to her signing an MGM contract in 1925. Garbo's luminous, romantic beauty and enigmatic presence combined to make her one of the icons of the silent era, her off-screen reclusiveness contributing to the legend. She made the transition to sound easily, her deep, husky voice enchanting audiences from her very first lines in *Anna Christie*. The 1930s brought a succession of hits that highlighted her timeless beauty, while her infectious outburst of laughter in *Ninotchka* became the film's selling point. Garbo retired in 1941 but continued to intrigue the public until her death in 1990.

Studio Portrait
(Warner Brothers 1942)
ph: Scotty Welbourne

Queen Christina
(MGM 1933)

KEY FILMS
Flesh and the Devil, 1926
Anna Christie, 1930
Mata Hari, 1931
Grand Hotel, 1932
Queen Christina, 1933
Anna Karenina, 1935
Camille, 1937
Conquest, 1937
Ninotchka, 1939
Two-Faced Woman, 1941

Ninotchka
with Melvyn Douglas
(MGM 1939)

"What, when drunk, one sees in other women, one sees in Garbo sober."

KENNETH TYNAN, CRITIC

Anna Karenina
(MGM 1935)
ph: C. S. Bull

Next page
Camille
with Robert Taylor
(MGM 1937)

AVA GARDNER

Ava Lavinia Gardner was born on Christmas Eve, 1922, in Grabtown, North Carolina, the daughter of a poor tobacco farmer. Her exquisite face got her a screen test, but she appeared in seventeen films before her sultry beauty in *The Killers* made her a screen goddess of the 1950s. Her marriages to Mickey Rooney, bandleader Artie Shaw, and Frank Sinatra grabbed the headlines, but Gardner was essentially a free spirit, a quality wonderfully captured in such films as *Mogambo* and *The Barefoot Contessa*. After divorcing Sinatra, she left Hollywood and lived briefly in Madrid before settling in London, where she died on Christmas Day, 1990.

Studio Portrait
(MGM 1949)
ph: Eric Carpenter

The Killers
(Universal 1946)
ph: Ray Jones

KEY FILMS
The Killers, 1946
One Touch of Venus, 1948
Pandora and the Flying
    Dutchman, 1951
Show Boat, 1951
The Snows of Kilimanjaro,
    1952
Mogambo, 1953
The Barefoot Contessa,
    1954
Bhowani Junction, 1956
The Sun Also Rises, 1957
On the Beach, 1958
55 Days at Peking, 1963
The Night of the Iguana,
    1964

**Pandora and the Flying
Dutchman**
with James Mason
(Romulus 1951)

The Barefoot Contessa
(United Artists 1954)

"What I'd really like to say about stardom is that it gave me everything I never wanted."

Mogambo
with Grace Kelly
(MGM 1953)

JUDY GARLAND

Acclaimed as one of the greatest entertainers of the twentieth century, Judy was born Frances Ethel Gumm in Grand Rapids, Michigan, on June 10, 1922, the youngest of three daughters of a show-biz couple. "Baby" Gumm made her stage debut at two, and very soon the Gumm Sisters were touring vaudeville. In movies by the time she was fourteen, Judy

Summer Stock
(MGM 1950)

film *The Wizard of Oz*. Judy's years at **MGM** were box-office gold for the studio, and her many concerts around the world left her adoring fans screaming for more. When she died of an accidental barbiturate overdose in London in 1969, she was barely forty-seven.

Studio Portrait
(MGM 1941)
ph: Eric Carpenter

KEY FILMS
The Wizard of Oz, 1939
Babes in Arms, 1939
Strike Up the Band, 1940
For Me and My Gal, 1942
Girl Crazy, 1942
Meet Me in St. Louis, 1944
The Clock, 1945
Easter Parade, 1948
Summer Stock, 1950
A Star Is Born, 1954
Judgment at Nuremberg,
    1960

The Wizard of Oz
(MGM 1939)

Babes on Broadway
with Mickey Rooney
(MGM 1941)

"She could turn a banal lyric into a little one-act drama that expressed a truth about human emotions."

SIR PETER HALL, DIRECTOR

A Star Is Born
with James Mason
(Warner Brothers 1954)

Meet Me in St. Louis
(MGM 1944)

RICHARD GERE

Richard Tiffany Gere was born on August 31, 1949, in Philadelphia. He became a proficient musician while still in school, debuting on the London stage in a production of *Grease*. Working in both theater and films, Gere made his breakthrough in *American Gigolo*, followed by *An Officer and a Gentleman*. His screen image established him as a powerful sex symbol for the 1980s, but he has since proven a serious actor as well as a deft romantic lead. His comedic talents were brought to the fore in the huge box-office success *Pretty Woman*, in which he partnered with the young Julia Roberts (the two had a "return engagement" in *Runaway Bride*). Gere is much respected for his strong support of many humanitarian causes.

Studio Portrait
(Touchstone 1990)

Pretty Woman
with Julia Roberts
(Touchstone 1990)

KEY FILMS
Looking for Mr. Goodbar, 1977
Days of Heaven, 1978
American Gigolo, 1980
An Officer and a Gentleman, 1982
Internal Affairs, 1990
Pretty Woman, 1990
Final Analysis, 1992
Sommersby, 1993
Red Corner, 1997
Runaway Bride, 1999
Chicago, 2002

American Gigolo
(Paramount 1980)
ph: Ron Grover

An Officer and a Gentleman
with Debra Winger
(Paramount 1982)
ph: Carol McCullough

*"The movie is the job and you do
the job the best you can."*

Primal Fear
(Paramount 1996)
ph: Ron Phillips

Red Corner
(MGM 1997)
ph: David James

MEL GIBSON

Although Mel Columcille Gerard Gibson was born in Peekskill, New York, on January 3, 1956, he grew up in Australia. There he began his acting career, and it was the highly successful *Mad Max* films that launched him internationally. His early American films displayed his considerable acting skills, although initially it may have been his boyishly handsome face that attracted his many female fans. With the *Lethal Weapon* series he became a top box-office draw, and as a major Hollywood star, he proved excellent in both light comedy and Shakespeare. Turning to directing as well as acting in the early 1990s, Gibson won an Academy Award as Best Director for *Braveheart*.

Studio Portrait
(Paramount/Icon 1998)
ph: Andrew Cooper

We Were Soldiers
(Paramount 2002)
ph: Stephen Vaughan

KEY FILMS
Mad Max, 1979
Gallipoli, 1981
Mad Max 2, 1981
The Year of Living
    Dangerously, 1982
The Bounty, 1984
Lethal Weapon, 1987
Hamlet, 1990
The Man Without a Face,
    1993 (also directed)
Braveheart, 1995
    (also directed)
What Women Want, 2000
Signs, 2002

"*You can't live up to what people expect.*
Nobody can. But I guess that's
my problem, not theirs."

**Mad Max: Beyond
Thunderdome**
(*Warner Brothers 1985*)
ph: Jim Sheldon

Lethal Weapon
(Warner Brothers 1987)
ph: John R. Shannon

Next page
Hamlet
(Paramount 1990)
ph: Keith Hamshere

What Women Want
(Paramount 2000)
ph: Andrew Cooper

Braveheart
(Icon/Ladd Co/Paramount
1995)
ph: Andrew Cooper

WHOOPI GOLDBERG

Whoopi Goldberg was born Caryn Elaine Johnson on November 13, 1955, in New York City, where she began performing as a child. Although she studied drama seriously, it was as a stand-up comic that she first made her mark. She toured her one-woman show and brought it to Broadway under the aegis of director Mike Nichols. Steven Spielberg's production of *The Color Purple* brought her an Academy Award nomination, and she won Best Supporting Actress for *Ghost*. She has since demonstrated her versatility in both serious drama and comedy and has also been a dazzling host for the annual Academy Awards ceremony.

Ghost
(Paramount 1990)
ph: Peter Sorel

Sister Act
(Touchstone 1992)
ph: Suzanne Hanover

KEY FILMS
The Color Purple, 1985
Clara's Heart, 1988
Ghost, 1990
The Player, 1992
Sister Act, 1992
Corrina, Corrina, 1994
Boys on the Side, 1995
Ghosts of Mississippi, 1996
The Deep End of the Ocean, 1999
Girl, Interrupted, 1999

"Actors have no color. That is the art form."

Corrina, Corrina
with Ray Liotta
(New Line 1994)
ph: Bonnie Schiffman

The Color Purple
(Warner Brothers 1985)
ph: John Shannon

CARY GRANT

Archibald Alexander Leach was born in Bristol, England, on January 18, 1904. Leaving school and an unstable home at fourteen, he toured as an acrobat, developing the grace and timing that would produce the most debonair and sophisticated leading man of his time. He appeared in several Hollywood films in the early 1930s and was launched as a star by

Studio Portrait
(Warner Brothers 1942)
ph: Scotty Welbourne

Mae West, who selected him as her leading man in *She Done Him Wrong*. He made over sixty films, including four with director Alfred Hitchcock, and worked with such leading ladies as Grace Kelly, Katharine Hepburn, Ingrid Bergman, and Audrey Hepburn. Grant received an honorary Academy Award in 1970. He died in 1986.

His Girl Friday
with Rosalind Russell
(Columbia 1940)
ph: A. L. "Whitey" Schafer

KEY FILMS
She Done Him Wrong, 1933
The Awful Truth, 1937
Bringing Up Baby, 1938
His Girl Friday, 1940
The Philadelphia Story, 1941
Suspicion, 1941
None but the Lonely Heart,
    1944
Notorious, 1946
I Was a Male War Bride,
    1949
To Catch a Thief, 1955
An Affair to Remember,
    1957
North by Northwest, 1959
Charade, 1963

The Bishop's Wife
(Goldwyn/RKO 1947)
ph: Ernest Bachrach

To Catch a Thief
with Grace Kelly
(Paramount 1955)
ph: Bud Fraker

Suspicion
(RKO 1941)

Arsenic and Old Lace
with Priscilla Lane
(Warner Brothers 1943)

"Everybody wants to be Cary Grant.
Even I want to be Cary Grant."

Next page
North by Northwest
with Eva Marie Saint
(MGM 1959)

GENE HACKMAN

Eugene Alden Hackman, born on January 30, 1930, in San Bernadino, California, joined the Marines when he was sixteen, and then took a variety of dead-end jobs until becoming an actor at thirty. Stage roles led to small film roles, until his breakthrough performance in *Bonnie and Clyde* brought him an Academy Award nomination. His performance as the tough cop

Bonnie and Clyde
(Warner Brothers 1967)

Popeye Doyle in *The French Connection* won him the Academy Award as Best Actor. One of Hollywood's finest, most versatile actors, he was nominated again for the harrowing *Mississippi Burning* and won a Best Supporting Actor for *Unforgiven*. Hackman has also revealed a talent for comedy, as his deliciously over-the-top Lex Luthor in *Superman* attests.

Crimson Tide
(Hollywood Pictures 1995)
ph: Richard Foreman

KEY FILMS
Bonnie and Clyde, 1967
The French Connection, 1971
The Poseidon Adventure, 1972
Scarecrow, 1973
The Conversation, 1974
Superman, 1978
Mississippi Burning, 1988
Unforgiven, 1992
Get Shorty, 1995
The Royal Tenenbaums, 2001

"If I start to become a star, I'll lose contact with the normal guys I play best."

The Royal Tenenbaums
(Touchstone 2001)
ph: James Hamilton

The French Connection
with José Fernandez
(20th Century Fox 1971)

TOM HANKS

Thomas J. Hanks was born in Concord, California, on July 9, 1956. His parents split up when he was five, and his childhood became a nomadic one. His first big acting break was co-starring in the TV sitcom *Bosom Buddies*, but it was with the film *Splash* that he became a major film actor. Now considered a superstar, his endearingly natural presence on screen produces films that are always big box-office hits. He is the first actor since Spencer Tracy to win back-to-back Academy Awards for Best Actor. Hanks won his awards for his roles in *Philadelphia* and *Forrest Gump*. In 2002 he became the youngest actor to be honored with the American Film Institute's Life Achievement Award.

Studio Portrait
(Warner Brothers 1998)
ph: Brian Hamill

The Green Mile
(Castle Rock/WB 1999)
ph: Ralph Nelson Jr.

KEY FILMS
Splash, 1984
Nothing in Common, 1986
Big, 1988
Sleepless in Seattle, 1993
Philadelphia, 1993
Forrest Gump, 1994
Apollo 13, 1995
That Thing You Do! 1996
    (also directed)
Saving Private Ryan, 1998
The Green Mile, 1999
Cast Away, 2000
Road to Perdition, 2002

Forrest Gump
(Paramount 1994)
ph: Phillip Caruso

Saving Private Ryan
(Dreamworks 1998)
ph: David James

Next page
Apollo 13
with Kevin Bacon
and Bill Paxton
(Universal 1995)
ph: Ron Batzdorff

"The guy who finds the
extraordinary in the ordinary."

MEG RYAN

Sleepless in Seattle
with Meg Ryan and
Ross Malinger
(Tri-Star 1993)
ph: Bruce McBroom

Cast Away
(Fox/Dreamworks 2000)
ph: Zade Rosenthal

JEAN HARLOW

Platinum blonde Jean Harlow was the major sex symbol of the 1930s. Born Harlean Harlow Carpenter in Kansas City, Missouri, on March 3, 1911, she worked as a film extra, then graduated to bit parts in comedy shorts before getting her breakthrough role in Howard Hughes's *Hell's Angels*. A contract with MGM produced a succession of good parts in which she could display both her blonde glamour and her innate talent for comedy, and she starred with some of the studio's top names. Harlow died in 1937 at twenty-six and was buried in the gown she wore in her final scene in *Saratoga*.

Studio Portrait
(MGM 1934)
ph: George Hurrell

Hold Your Man
with Clark Gable
(MGM 1933)

KEY FILMS
Hell's Angels, 1930
The Public Enemy, 1931
Platinum Blonde, 1931
Red-Headed Woman, 1932
Red Dust, 1932
Bombshell, 1933
Dinner at Eight, 1934
Wife vs. Secretary, 1936
Libeled Lady, 1936
Saratoga, 1937

"*Jean Harlow was very soft about her toughness.*"

GEORGE CUKOR,
DIRECTOR

The Beast of the City
(MGM 1932)

Personal Property
with Robert Taylor
(MGM 1937)
ph: Ted Allan

Next page
Platinum Blonde
(Columbia 1931)

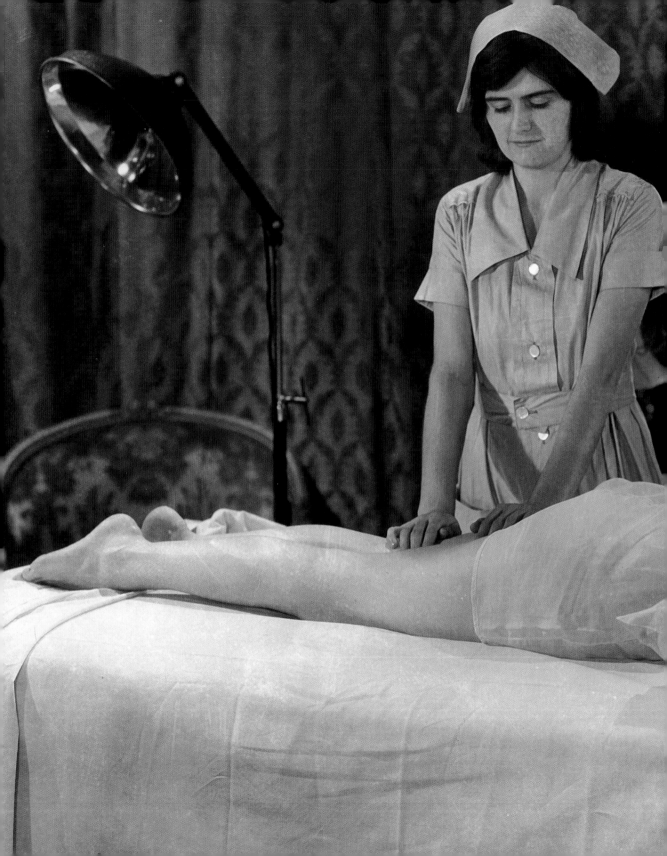

RITA HAYWORTH

Rita Hayworth was born Margarita Carmen Cansino in Brooklyn, New York, on October 17, 1918. A professional dancer at twelve and a film actress at sixteen, Rita became a top star at Columbia Pictures. Labeled "Hollywood's Love Goddess," she was a favorite G.I. pin-up during World War II.

Her first postwar film, *Gilda*, was a classic film noir and a spectacular success. In it she encapsulates the spirit of both the vamp and the lovelorn beauty. None of her five marriages, including those to Orson Welles and Prince Aly Khan, proved to be happy. She died of Alzheimer's disease in 1987.

Studio Portrait
(Columbia 1944)
ph: Robert Coburn

Pal Joey
(Columbia 1957)

KEY FILMS
Only Angels Have Wings, 1939
The Strawberry Blonde, 1941
You'll Never Get Rich, 1941
Blood and Sand, 1941
Cover Girl, 1944
Gilda, 1946
The Lady from Shanghai, 1948
Salome, 1953
Miss Sadie Thompson, 1953
Pal Joey, 1957
Separate Tables, 1958

"Her essential quality was sweetness. There was a richness of texture about her that was very interesting and very unlike a movie star."

ORSON WELLES

Gilda
(Columbia 1946)

Cover Girl
(Columbia 1944)
ph: Robert Coburn

Next page
The Lady from Shanghai
with Orson Welles
(Columbia 1948)

AUDREY HEPBURN

Sabrina
(Paramount 1954)
ph: Bud Fraker

Audrey Hepburn was born Edda van Heemstra Hepburn-Ruston in Brussels, Belgium, on May 4, 1929. She suffered the privations of World War II, coming to London after the war to seek work in the theater. Small roles in British films led to her discovery by director William Wyler, who cast her as a rebellious princess in *Roman Holiday*, opposite Gregory Peck. Her charm and elegance captivated a worldwide public, and she won an Academy Award as Best Actress for her role. Throughout her film career Hepburn starred with some of the greatest leading men of the screen. In her later years she worked tirelessly as a roving ambassador for UNICEF. She died in 1993.

Roman Holiday
(Paramount 1953)

KEY FILMS
Roman Holiday, 1953
Sabrina, 1954
Funny Face, 1957
Love in the Afternoon, 1957
The Nun's Story, 1959
Breakfast at Tiffany's, 1961
Charade, 1963
My Fair Lady, 1964
Two for the Road, 1967
Wait Until Dark, 1967

YИAᖷᖷIT

Breakfast at Tiffany's
with George Peppard
*(Paramount, Jurow-Shepherd
1961)*

My Fair Lady
(Warner Brothers 1964)

Next page
Sabrina
(Paramount 1954)
ph: Bud Fraker

"Audrey had grace and manners—
things you cannot take a
course in. God kissed her on the
cheek and there she was."

BILLY WILDER, DIRECTOR

Two for the Road
with Albert Finney
(20th Century Fox 1967)

Funny Face
(Paramount 1957)
ph: Richard Avedon

KATHARINE HEPBURN

One of the finest actresses of the screen and a true original, Katharine Hepburn was born on November 9, 1907, in Hartford, Connecticut. She was drawn to acting at an early age and began her career on the stage, winning an RKO contract in 1932 on the strength of a Broadway success. She won an Academy Award for her third film, *Morning Glory,* and built her subsequent career both on the stage and in film. Her partnership with Spencer Tracy, on and off screen, began with *Woman of the Year* and included nine films. The last movie they made together before Tracy died was *Guess Who's Coming to Dinner,* for which Hepburn won her second Academy Award. A third Academy Award came the next year with *The Lion in Winter,* and she won her fourth for *On Golden Pond.* Hepburn's unique blend of strength and tenderness brought her eight other Academy Award nominations. She passed away at her Connecticut home in 2003. She was 96.

Studio Portrait
(RKO 1935)
ph: Ernest Bachrach

The Lion in Winter
(Avco/Embassy 1968)

KEY FILMS
A Bill of Divorcement, 1932
Morning Glory, 1933
Little Women, 1933
Alice Adams, 1935
Bringing Up Baby, 1938
The Philadelphia Story, 1940
Woman of the Year, 1942
Adam's Rib, 1949
The African Queen, 1951
Summertime, 1955
Suddenly Last Summer, 1959
Long Day's Journey into Night, 1962
Guess Who's Coming to Dinner, 1967
The Lion in Winter, 1968
On Golden Pond, 1981

The Philadelphia Story
with James Stewart
(MGM 1940)
ph: James Manatt

Summertime
with Rossano Brazzi
(United Artists 1955)

*"I always wanted
to be a movie actress.
I thought it was
very romantic.
And it was."*

Bringing Up Baby
(RKO 1938)

CHARLTON HESTON

Charlton Heston was born John Charles Carter on October 4, 1924, in Evanston, Illinois. He studied drama at Northwestern University, served in the Air Corps in World War II, then made his Broadway debut in 1947, which was soon followed by roles in the movies. His strong physicality made him a natural screen hero. Leading roles in some of the most spectacular films of the day included, memorably, Moses in *The Ten Commandments* and the title role in *Ben-Hur*, for which he won the Academy Award as Best Actor. In his long career he has continued to dominate the screen in a wide variety of roles as well as appearing in many distinguished stage productions. The Academy also gave him its Humanitarian Award in 1977.

Studio Portrait
(Paramount 1958)

The Ten Commandments
(Paramount 1956)

KEY FILMS
The Greatest Show on
   Earth, 1952
The Ten Commandments,
   1956
Touch of Evil, 1958
The Big Country, 1958
Ben-Hur, 1959
El Cid, 1961
55 Days at Peking, 1963
The Agony and the Ecstasy,
   1965
Khartoum, 1966
Planet of the Apes, 1970
Earthquake, 1974

"*That guy Heston has to watch it. If he's not careful, he'll give actors a good name.*"

FRANK SINATRA

Ben-Hur
with Stephen Boyd
(*MGM 1959*)

Touch of Evil
with Janet Leigh
(*Universal 1958*)

The Agony and the Ecstasy
(20th Century Fox 1965)

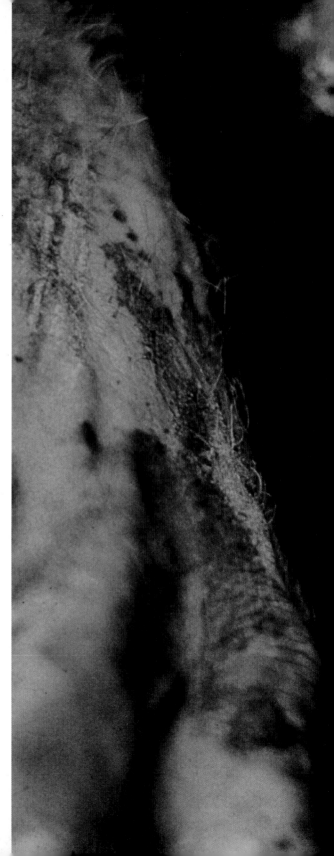

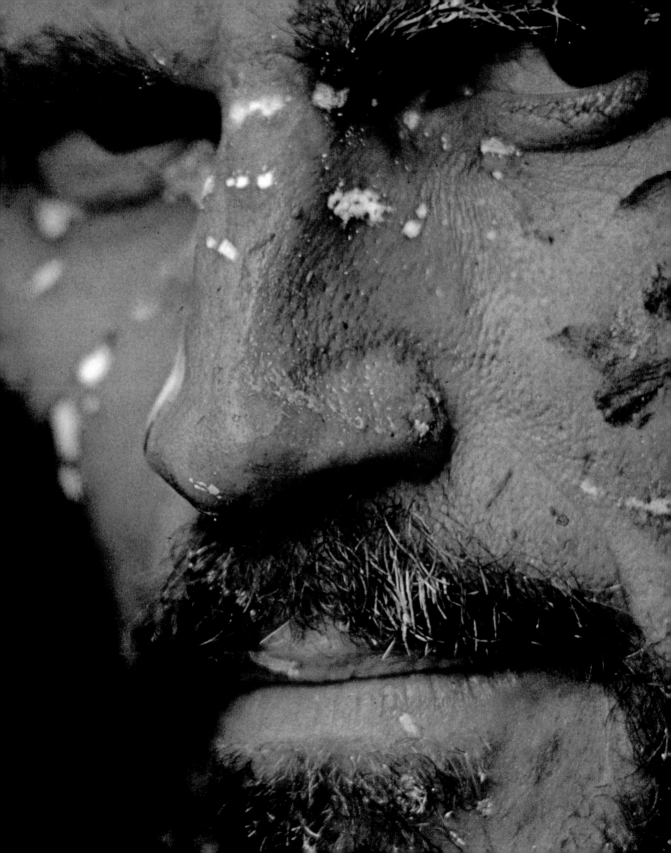

DUSTIN HOFFMAN

Studio Portrait
(Columbia 1979)

Born in Los Angeles on August 8, 1937, Dustin Lee Hoffman has shown a remarkable ability to play a wide range of roles. His work on the stage in New York caught the attention of director Mike Nichols, who cast him in the film *The Graduate*, making Hoffman an instant hero for the 1960s generation. His subsequent roles have been astonishingly varied from the street urchin in *Midnight Cowboy* to the alternative comedian Lenny Bruce in *Lenny*. Hoffman won Academy Awards as the desperate single parent in *Kramer vs. Kramer* and for his touching portrayal of Tom Cruise's autistic brother in *Rain Man*, and he has received five other Academy Award nominations.

Tootsie
(Columbia 1982)

KEY FILMS
The Graduate, 1967
Midnight Cowboy, 1969
Papillon, 1973
Lenny, 1974
All the President's Men,
     1976
Marathon Man, 1976
Kramer vs. Kramer, 1979
Tootsie, 1982
Rain Man, 1988
Wag the Dog, 1997

Midnight Cowboy
(United Artists 1969)

"I lived below the official American poverty line until I was 31."

The Graduate
(Embassy 1967)

Rain Man
with Tom Cruise
(United Artists 1988)
ph: Stephen Vaughan

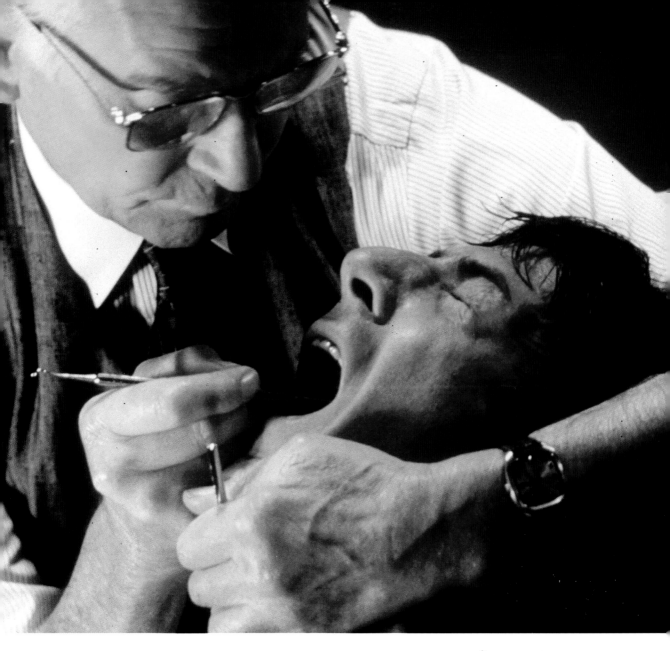

Marathon Man
with Laurence Olivier
(Paramount 1976)
ph: Peter Sorel

BOB HOPE

Leslie Townes Hope was born on May 29, 1903, in Eltham, England, and raised in Cleveland, Ohio. Hope's career has spanned three-quarters of a century. He has been a star in vaudeville, on Broadway, and on radio and television as well as in films. The seven Road pictures he made with Bing Crosby and Dorothy Lamour have been particular audience pleasers, but he also held his own against Jane Russell in *The Paleface* and Lucille Ball in *Fancy Pants*. He is admired for his countless overseas trips to entertain American forces and has received five Academy Awards for his humanitarian work. Queen Elizabeth bestowed an honorary knighthood on Hope in 1998.

Studio Portrait
(Paramount 1944)
ph: A. L. "Whitey" Schafer

The Paleface
with Jane Russell
(Paramount 1948)

KEY FILMS
The Cat and the Canary,
   1938
Road to Singapore, 1940
Road to Zanzibar, 1941
My Favorite Blonde, 1942
The Princess and the Pirate,
   1944
Monsieur Beaucaire, 1946
The Paleface, 1948
Sorrowful Jones, 1948
Fancy Pants, 1950
The Seven Little Foys, 1954
The Facts of Life, 1960

"They said I was worth $500 million. If I was worth that much, I wouldn't have visited Vietnam, I'd have sent for it."

The Ghost Breakers
with Paulette Goddard
(Paramount 1940)
ph: A. L. "Whitey" Schafer

Road to Zanzibar
with Bing Crosby and
Dorothy Lamour
(Paramount 1941)

ROCK HUDSON

Tall, dark, and handsome Roy Harold Scherer Jr. was born in Winnetka, Illinois, on November 17, 1925. He served as a Navy mechanic during World War II, and when he hit Hollywood he became one of the last young actors whose career was developed under the studio system. Bit parts and supporting roles led to major stardom as a romantic leading man.

Hudson was nominated for an Academy Award for *Giant*, and he was a perfect comic foil to Doris Day in *Pillow Talk*. In later years he starred in the highly successful TV series *MacMillan and Wife* and also appeared in *Dynasty*. Hudson was the first international celebrity whose death, in 1985, was attributed to AIDS.

Studio Portrait
(Universal 1951)
ph: Sherman Clark

Magnificent Obsession
with Jane Wyman
(Universal 1954)

KEY FILMS
Magnificent Obsession, 1954
All That Heaven Allows, 1955
Giant, 1956
Written on the Wind, 1956
A Farewell to Arms, 1957
The Tarnished Angels, 1957
Pillow Talk, 1959
Lover Come Back, 1961
Seconds, 1966
The Mirror Crack'd, 1980

"*He will always be remembered for his dynamic impact on the film industry.*"

RONALD REAGAN

A Farewell to Arms
with Jennifer Jones
(20th Century Fox 1957)

Pillow Talk
with Doris Day
(Universal 1959)

SAMUEL L. JACKSON

Samuel Leroy Jackson was born on December 21, 1948, in Washington, D.C., and raised in a single parent family. He worked at many jobs in New York before joining the famed Negro Ensemble Company. His breakthrough to stardom came in Spike Lee's *Jungle Fever*, playing a drug addict. He had publicly overcome his own drug problem and declared that, in doing so, he found his true strength as an actor. A part written for him by Quentin Tarentino for *Pulp Fiction* earned Jackson an Academy Award nomination, and he has since blazed across the screen in a wide variety of demanding and dramatic roles. Known as the "king of cool," he has expressed great delight at the opportunity to appear in the *Star Wars* prequels.

The Negotiator
(Monarchy/Regency 1998)
ph: Sam Emerson

Shaft
(Paramount 2000)
ph: Eli Reed

KEY FILMS
Jungle Fever, 1991
Jurassic Park, 1993
Pulp Fiction, 1994
Die Hard: With a
  Vengeance, 1995
A Time to Kill, 1996
Eve's Bayou, 1997
  (also produced)
Jackie Brown, 1997
Star Wars: Episode I –
  The Phantom Menace,
  1999
Rules of Engagement, 2000
Shaft, 2000
Star Wars: Episode II –
  Attack of the Clones,
  2002
Changing Lanes, 2002

"*I was a square for so long and it totally amazes me that people think I am cool.*"

A Time to Kill
with Matthew McConaughey
(*Warner Brothers 1996*)
ph: Christine Loss

Jackie Brown
with Pam Grier
(Miramax 1997)
ph: Darren Michaels

TOMMY LEE JONES

Born in San Saba, Texas, on September 5, 1946, Tommy Lee Jones won a scholarship to Harvard University, where his roommate was the future Vice President Al Gore. He worked on the New York stage and in television soap operas before getting noticed in Roger Corman's film *Jackson County Jail*. Stardom was assured by his electrifying portrayal of convicted killer Gary Gilmore in the television drama *The Executioner's Song*, and major film roles followed. Jones won an Academy Award as Best Supporting Actor for *The Fugitive* and has forged a memorable comic partnership with Will Smith in the *Men in Black* films.

Men in Black
(Columbia 1997)
ph: Michael O' Neill

The Fugitive
(Warner Brothers 1993)
ph: Stephen Vaughan

KEY FILMS
Jackson County Jail, 1976
Coal Miner's Daughter, 1980
JFK, 1991
The Fugitive, 1993
The Client, 1994
Cobb, 1994
Men in Black, 1997
Rules of Engagement, 2000
Men in Black 2, 2002

The River Rat
(Paramount 1984)

"It's no mean calling to bring fun into the afternoons of large numbers of people."

Coal Miner's Daughter
with Sissy Spacek
(Universal 1980)

GENE KELLY

The superb dancer and choreographer Eugene Curran Kelly was born in Pittsburgh on August 23, 1912. Playing the title role in *Pal Joey* on Broadway in 1940 brought him stage stardom, and his screen debut came two years later, when he starred opposite Judy Garland in *For Me and My Gal*. Kelly's charm and natural screen presence powered his relaxed dancing style, bringing a new freshness to the movie musical. His innovations included dancing with cartoon characters in *Anchors Aweigh* and the use of real locations for dance sequences in *On the Town*. He co-directed three films with Stanley Donen during the heyday of the MGM musical and continued to direct until his death in 1996.

Studio Portrait
(MGM 1953)
ph: Virgil Apger

It's Always Fair Weather
with Cyd Charisse
(MGM 1955)
ph: Virgil Apger

KEY FILMS
For Me and My Gal, 1942
Cover Girl, 1944
Anchors Aweigh, 1945
Take Me Out to the Ball
    Game, 1949
On the Town, 1949 (also
    co-directed)
Summer Stock, 1950
An American in Paris, 1951
Singin' in the Rain, 1952
    (also co-directed)
It's Always Fair Weather,
    1955 (also co-directed)
Invitation to the Dance,
    1956 (also directed)
Inherit the Wind, 1960

Singin' in the Rain
(MGM 1952)

An American in Paris
with Leslie Caron
(MGM 1951)
ph: C. S. Bull

On the Town
with Vera-Ellen
(MGM 1949)

Anchors Aweigh
with Frank Sinatra
(MGM 1945)

"I never wanted to be a dancer. It's true! I wanted to be a shortstop for the Pittsburgh Pirates."

Brigadoon
with Cyd Charisse
(MGM 1954)

GRACE KELLY

Grace Patricia Kelly was born in Philadelphia on November 12, 1929. Her classic beauty helped her into a successful modeling career, and she had appeared on many fashion magazine covers when Hollywood beckoned. A small role in *Fourteen Hours* (1951) led to a part opposite Gary Cooper in the Academy Award–winning *High Noon*. In less than six years she appeared in eleven films, including three directed by Alfred Hitchcock. She won an Academy Award as Best Actress in *The Country Girl*, playing the downtrodden wife of an alcoholic actor. While filming *To Catch a Thief* on the Riviera, she met Prince Rainier of Monaco, whom she married in 1956. Princess Grace died tragically in an automobile accident in 1982.

Studio Portrait
(Paramount 1955)
ph: Bud Fraker

High Society
(MGM 1956)

KEY FILMS
High Noon, 1952
Mogambo, 1952
Dial M for Murder, 1954
Rear Window, 1954
The Country Girl, 1954
To Catch a Thief, 1955
High Society, 1956

"What man wouldn't be overwhelmed by her?"

WILLIAM HOLDEN

To Catch a Thief
(Paramount 1955)
ph: Bud Fraker

High Noon
(Stanley Kramer/UA 1952)

Next page
Rear Window
with James Stewart
(Paramount 1954)

NICOLE KIDMAN

Although Nicole Mary Kidman was born in Honolulu, Hawaii, on June 20, 1967, she is in fact Australian. She made her first film at fourteen, starred on Australian television, and came to Hollywood to appear in *Days of Thunder* opposite Tom Cruise, whom she subsequently married. Her career took off with *To Die For* in which her deft characterization as a murderous weathergirl was highly praised. While in London to make Stanley Kubrick's last film, *Eyes Wide Shut*, the tall, red-haired Kidman had a wild success on the stage in *The Blue Room* and she subsequently repeated her performance on Broadway. Kidman has proved her versatility in roles as disparate as the repressed mother in the ghost story *The Others* and as the consumptive showgirl in *Moulin Rouge*. She went on to win the Academy Award as Best Actress for her engaging role in *The Hours*.

Eyes Wide Shut
with Tom Cruise
(Warner Brothers 1999)

KEY FILMS
Dead Calm, 1989
Days of Thunder, 1990
Far and Away, 1992
To Die For, 1995
The Portrait of a Lady, 1996
Eyes Wide Shut, 1999
Moulin Rouge, 2001
The Others, 2001
Birthday Girl, 2001
The Hours, 2002

Moulin Rouge
(20th Century Fox 2001)
ph: Sue Adler

To Die For
with Matt Dillon
(Columbia 1995)
ph: Kerry Hayes

The Hours
(Miramax 2002)

"Even from a very early age I knew I didn't want to miss out on anything life had to offer just because it might be considered dangerous."

BURT LANCASTER

Burton Stephen Lancaster grew up on the tough streets of New York City, where he was born on November 2, 1913. He dropped out of college to form an acrobatics team and worked at dead-end jobs before serving in World War II. A talent scout spotted him in a Broadway play, and he made his screen debut in *The Killers*, immediately achieving stardom. A handsome, dazzlingly physical actor, he excelled in solid dramatic roles, winning an Academy Award for *Elmer Gantry*. He frequently worked with top foreign directors and later formed his own production company, which provided him with some of his greatest successes. He died in 1994.

Studio Portrait
(Paramount 1948)
ph: Mal Bulloch

Gunfight at the O.K. Corral
with Kirk Douglas
(Paramount 1957)

KEY FILMS
The Killers, 1946
Sorry, Wrong Number, 1948
The Crimson Pirate, 1952
Come Back, Little Sheba, 1952
From Here to Eternity, 1953
The Rose Tattoo, 1955
Gunfight at the O.K. Corral, 1957
Sweet Smell of Success, 1957
Elmer Gantry, 1960
Birdman of Alcatraz, 1962
The Professionals, 1966
Atlantic City, 1980

The Crimson Pirate
(Warner Brothers 1952)

Elmer Gantry
(United Artists 1960)

Next page
From Here to Eternity
with Deborah Kerr
(Columbia 1953)

*"We're all forgotten sooner or later.
But not films. That's all the memorial we
should need or hope for."*

VIVIEN LEIGH

Vivian Mary Hartley was born on November 5, 1913, in Darjeeling, India, where her father was a businessman. Appearances on the London stage and in British films made her lovely face well known before she starred opposite Laurence Olivier in *Fire over England*. Leigh and Oliver began a romance that made headlines on both sides of the Atlantic before marrying in 1940. Famously cast as the lead in *Gone with the Wind* when she was

A Streetcar Named Desire
with Marlon Brando
(Warner Brothers 1951)

spotted on the set watching the burning of Atlanta sequence, she won an Academy Award for the role of Scarlett O'Hara. Another Best Actress award came for her touching portrayal of Blanche in *A Streetcar Named Desire*. She played many major Shakespearean roles opposite Olivier before their divorce. She died in 1967.

Studio Portrait
(MGM 1940)
ph: Laszlo Willinger

KEY FILMS
Fire over England, 1937
A Yank at Oxford, 1938
Gone with the Wind, 1939
Waterloo Bridge, 1940
That Hamilton Woman, 1941
Caesar and Cleopatra, 1945
A Streetcar Named Desire,
   1951
The Roman Spring of
   Mrs. Stone, 1961
Ship of Fools, 1965

A Yank at Oxford
with Robert Taylor
(MGM 1938)

Waterloo Bridge
(MGM 1940)
ph: Laszlo Willinger

*"She'd have
crawled over
broken glass if
she thought it
would help her
performance."*

ELIA KAZAN
DIRECTOR

Gone with the Wind
(Selznick/MGM 1939)

SOPHIA LOREN

ofia Villani Scicolone was born on September 30, 1934, in Puzzuoli, Italy. She grew up in poverty on the streets of Naples, and as her beauty and natural assets developed, she began to land small movie roles. Her mentor, producer Carlo Ponti, whom she married in 1957, managed her career in Italian films, building her into a star. Hollywood soon discovered the voluptuous Loren and teamed her with its top leading men. She proved herself as adept in romantic comedy as in dramatic roles. She won the Best Actress award for *Two Women*, making her the first performer acting in a foreign language to win an Academy Award. Loren moves easily between Hollywood and Italy and has succeeded in raising her two children out of the glare of publicity.

Studio Portrait
(Paramount 1958)
ph: Bud Fraker

Boy on a Dolphin
(20th Century Fox 1957)

KEY FILMS
The Pride and the Passion, 1957
Houseboat, 1958
It Started in Naples, 1960
Two Women (La Ciociara), 1960
El Cid, 1961
The Fall of the Roman Empire, 1964
Arabesque, 1966
Man of La Mancha, 1972
Prêt-à-Porter, 1994
Grumpier Old Men, 1995

"Sex appeal is 50 percent what you've got and 50 percent what people think you've got."

Heller in Pink Tights
(Paramount 1960)

Houseboat
with Cary Grant
(Paramount 1958)

The Fall of the Roman Empire
with Alec Guinness
(Samuel Bronston 1964)

STEVE McQUEEN

Terrence Steven McQueen was born on March 24, 1930, in Beech Grove, Indiana. When he was a baby, his father deserted the family, and McQueen grew up wild and independent. After three years in the Marines he tried his luck in New York as an actor, studying at the famous Actor's Studio. The leading role in a low-budget horror film, *The Blob*, got him noticed, and his part in *The Magnificent Seven* made him a star. By 1970 his maverick persona had established him as one of the top movie stars in the world. He died of cancer in 1980.

Studio Portrait
(1968)

The Magnificent Seven
(United Artists 1960)

KEY FILMS
The Magnificent Seven, 1960
The Great Escape, 1963
Love with the Proper Stranger, 1963
The Cincinnati Kid, 1965
The Sand Pebbles, 1966
The Thomas Crown Affair, 1968
Bullitt, 1968
The Getaway, 1972
Papillon, 1973
The Towering Inferno, 1974

*"If I hadn't made it
as an actor, I might have
wound up a hood."*

Bullitt
(Warner Brothers 1968)

The Great Escape
(Mirisch/UA 1963)

The Thomas Crown Affair
with Faye Dunaway
(United Artists 1968)

Papillon
(Allied Artists 1973)

The Cincinnati Kid
(MGM 1965)

ROBERT MITCHUM

El Dorado
(Paramount 1967)

Robert Charles Durman Mitchum was born in Bridgeport, Connecticut, on August 6, 1917. He ran away from home as a teenager and worked at a variety of jobs all over the States until he began acting, playing small film roles in Hollywood in 1943 before serving in World War II. His breakthrough role in *The Story of G.I. Joe* brought him an Academy Award nomination. Mitchum's public "bad boy" image often detracted from his solid acting talent, and he performed in such differing roles as the terrifying villain in *The Night of the Hunter* and the gentle schoolteacher in *Ryan's Daughter*. Mitchum died in 1997.

Studio Portrait
(RKO 1950)
ph: Ernest Bachrach

KEY FILMS
The Story of G.I. Joe, 1945
Out of the Past, 1947
The Big Steal, 1949
River of No Return, 1954
The Night of the Hunter, 1955
Heaven Knows, Mr. Allison, 1957
The Wonderful Country, 1959
The Sundowners, 1960
Cape Fear, 1962
El Dorado, 1967
Ryan's Daughter, 1970
The Friends of Eddie Coyle, 1973

"It sure beats working."

The Night of the Hunter
(United Artists 1955)

Cape Fear
(Universal 1962)

His Kind of Woman
with Jane Russell
(RKO 1951)

Heaven Knows, Mr. Allison
with Deborah Kerr
(20th Century Fox 1957)

MARILYN MONROE

Arguably the most famous movie star ever, Norma Jean Mortensen was born in Los Angeles on June 1, 1926. Her mother was mentally unstable and abandoned her to a series of foster homes. As a teenager, Monroe became a swimsuit model competing in many local beauty contests. Her rise to film stardom began slowly with small parts until, suddenly, it was meteoric. Everyone in the world knew which blonde gentlemen preferred. Her marriages to baseball legend Joe DiMaggio and distinguished playwright Arthur Miller were unsuccessful. Although Marilyn died at the age of thirty-six in 1962, she remains—nearly half a century later—an icon whose luster has never diminished.

Studio Portrait
(20th Century Fox 1951)

Some Like it Hot
with Tony Curtis
(United Artists 1959)
ph: Bernie Abramson

KEY FILMS
The Asphalt Jungle, 1950
Niagara, 1952
Gentlemen Prefer Blondes, 1953
How to Marry a Millionaire, 1953
There's No Business Like Show Business, 1954
The Seven Year Itch, 1955
Bus Stop, 1956
Some Like It Hot, 1959
Let's Make Love, 1960
The Misfits, 1961

How to Marry a Millionaire
with Cameron Mitchell
(20th Century Fox 1953)

*"Sex is part of nature and
I go along with nature."*

River of No Return
(20th Century Fox 1954)

Next page
Niagara
(20th Century Fox 1952)

Gentlemen Prefer Blondes
with Jane Russell and
Charles Coburn
(20th Century Fox 1953)

The Seven Year Itch
with Tom Ewell
(20th Century Fox 1955)

EDDIE MURPHY

Edward Regan Murphy was born in Brooklyn, New York, on April 3, 1961. He got his start as a stand-up comic, progressing via the popular television show *Saturday Night Live* to a film contract. His debut film, *48 Hrs.*, hit box-office gold, and Murphy was soon a top movie name. The *Beverly Hills Cop* series followed, capitalizing on his easy-going screen persona and adroit comic timing. He has since directed, produced, and starred in *Harlem Nights* and remade both *The Nutty Professor* and *Doctor Dolittle* in his own inimitable style. His witty voice as the donkey in the Academy Award—winning *Shrek* was a major factor in the film's wide appeal.

48 Hrs.
with Nick Nolte
(Paramount 1982)
ph: Bruce McBroom

KEY FILMS
48 Hrs., 1982
Trading Places, 1983
Beverly Hills Cop, 1984
Coming to America, 1988
Harlem Nights, 1990 (also
    directed and produced)
Boomerang, 1992
The Nutty Professor, 1996
Doctor Dolittle, 1998
Bowfinger, 1999
Shrek, 2001

Beverly Hills Cop
(Paramount 1984)
ph: Richard R Robinson

Trading Places
(Paramount 1983)
ph: Josh Weiner

Coming to America
with Arsenio Hall
(Paramount 1988)
ph: John Seakwood

"I started out as an impressionist and that's all about observing—how people move, their voice quality, their attitudes and quirks."

Doctor Dolittle
(20th Century Fox 1998)
ph: Phil Bray

The Nutty Professor
(Universal 1996)
ph: Bruce McBroom

PAUL NEWMAN

A major star for almost half a century, Paul Leonard Newman was born in Shaker Heights, Ohio, on November 26, 1925. After serving in the Navy he studied at the Actors Studio and appeared on Broadway. Newman's first film, *The Silver Chalice* (1954), propelled him to stardom. His handsome, chiseled features and blue eyes combined with a strong screen presence have produced many memorable performances in award-winning movies, although his own Best Actor Academy Award came relatively late with *The Color of Money*. Newman's first directorial effort, *Rachel, Rachel*, starred his wife Joanne Woodward, and he has since directed five additional films. His "Newman's Own" food products have earned more than $100 million for children's charities.

Studio Portrait
(MGM 1955)
ph: Eric Carpenter

Cool Hand Luke
(Warner Brothers 1967)

KEY FILMS
Somebody Up There Likes
    Me, 1956
The Long Hot Summer, 1958
Cat on a Hot Tin Roof, 1958
Exodus, 1960
The Hustler, 1961
Sweet Bird of Youth, 1962
Hud, 1963
Cool Hand Luke, 1967
Rachel, Rachel, 1968
Butch Cassidy and the
    Sundance Kid, 1969
The Sting, 1973
The Verdict, 1982
The Color of Money, 1986
Road to Perdition, 2002

A New Kind of Love
with Joanne Woodward
(Paramount 1963)

"I really just can't watch myself.
I see all the machinery at work and
it just drives me nuts."

Butch Cassidy and the Sundance Kid
(20th Century Fox 1969)

The Hustler
(20th Century Fox 1961)

Hud
with Brandon De Wilde
(Paramount 1963)

Harper
(Warner Brothers 1966)

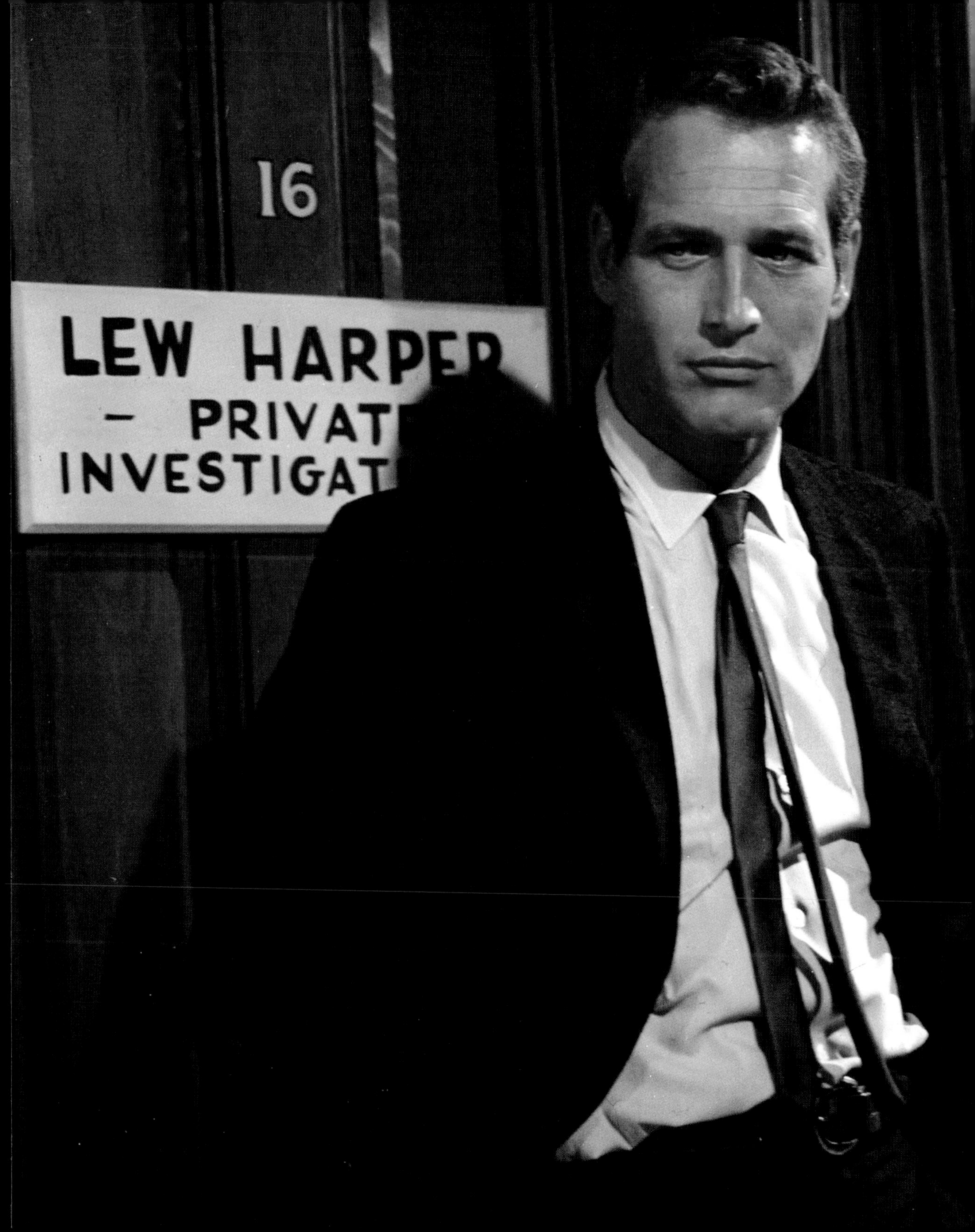
16
LEW HARPER
- PRIVAT
INVESTIGAT

JACK NICHOLSON

Jack Nicholson, born John Joseph Nicholson on April 22, 1937, in Neptune, New Jersey, is unquestionably one of the finest actors on the American screen. His first role was in Roger Corman's *The Cry Baby Killer* (1958). He made several more low-budget features—often co-writing or co-producing—before getting his big break in *Easy Rider*. Nicholson's ascent to major stardom was swift, crowned by a Best Actor Academy Award for his bravura performance in *One Flew Over the Cuckoo's Nest*. Never less than riveting on screen and often reaching greatness, Nicholson has had eight Academy Award nominations, won his second Best Actor award for *As Good As It Gets*, and also received one for Best Supporting Actor for *Terms of Endearment*.

Studio Portrait
(1983)

Chinatown
(Paramount 1974)

KEY FILMS
Easy Rider, 1969
Five Easy Pieces, 1970
Carnal Knowledge, 1971
The Last Detail, 1973
Chinatown, 1974
One Flew Over the Cuckoo's Nest, 1975
The Shining, 1980
The Postman Always Rings Twice, 1981
Reds, 1981
Terms of Endearment, 1985
Prizzi's Honor, 1985
As Good As It Gets, 1997
About Schmidt, 2002

**One Flew Over the
Cuckoo's Nest**
with Will Sampson
(United Artists 1975)
ph: Peter Sorel

Five Easy Pieces
(Columbia 1970)
ph: Bernie Abramson

As Good As It Gets
(Tri-Star 1997)
ph: Ralph Nelson Jr.

"If you're lucky enough to have a career as an actor, it becomes vital to save your own life inside that."

**The Postman Always
Rings Twice**
with Jessica Lange
(Paramount 1981)
ph: Carol McCullough

Next page
The Shining
with Shelley Duvall
(Warner Brothers 1980)

KIM NOVAK

Marilyn Pauline Novak was born in Chicago on February 13, 1933. A successful teenage model, she was put under contract by Columbia Pictures as their answer to 20th Century Fox's Marilyn Monroe. The camera loved Novak's luscious beauty, and she soon gained the acting skills required to earn the respect of her peers as well as develop a major fan base. During twenty years of stardom she appeared with some of Hollywood's top leading men, most memorably Frank Sinatra in *The Man with the Golden Arm* and in two films with James Stewart.

Studio Portrait
(Columbia 1956)
ph: Robert Coburn

Vertigo
(Paramount 1958)

KEY FILMS
Pushover, 1954
Picnic, 1955
The Man with the Golden
    Arm, 1956
Jeanne Eagles, 1957
Pal Joey, 1958
Vertigo, 1958
Bell Book and Candle, 1958
Middle of the Night, 1959
Of Human Bondage, 1964
Kiss Me, Stupid, 1964
The Mirror Crack'd, 1980

Kiss Me, Stupid
(United Artists 1964)

"*Very few American actresses are quite as carnal on the screen.*"

FRANÇOIS TRUFFAUT, DIRECTOR

Picnic
with William Holden
(Columbia 1955)
ph: Robert Coburn

AL PACINO

Alfredo James Pacino was born in New York City on April 25, 1940. Early stage experience, study at the Actors Studio, and the part of a heroin addict in the film *Panic in Needle Park* (1971) brought him to the attention of Francis Ford Coppola, who cast him as Marlon Brando's son in *The Godfather*. Pacino's powerfully subtle performance won him an Academy Award nomination, the first of several. He finally won the Academy Award as Best Actor for *Scent of a Woman*, playing a blind, embittered former soldier. Pacino's handsome and brooding presence is mesmerizing on the screen. He is both a true star and a great actor, infusing all of his roles, comic or dramatic, with an amazing truthfulness.

Studio Portrait
(1990)

Dog Day Afternoon
(Warner Brothers 1975)
ph: Muky

KEY FILMS
The Godfather, 1972
Scarecrow, 1973
Serpico, 1973
The Godfather, Part II, 1974
Dog Day Afternoon, 1975
Scarface, 1983
Dick Tracy, 1990
Scent of a Woman, 1992
Carlito's Way, 1993
Heat, 1995
Donnie Brasco, 1997
Any Given Sunday, 1999
Insomnia, 2002

Heat
(Monarchy/Regency 1995)
ph: Frank Connor

The Godfather, Part II
with John Cazale
(Paramount 1974)

"Whenever I get the urge to exercise,
I lie down until it passes."

Scarface
with Steven Bauer
(Universal 1983)
ph: Sidney Baldwin

Any Given Sunday
(Warner Brothers 1999)
ph: Robert Zuckerman

GWYNETH PALTROW

The daughter of show business parents, Gwyneth Kate Paltrow was born in Los Angeles on September 28, 1972, and grew up in New York. After dropping out of college, she was cast in several small film roles before playing Brad Pitt's wife in *Seven*. The title role of the Jane Austen heroine, *Emma*, gave her the opportunity to display her perfect English accent, which she employed once again in *Shakespeare in Love*, for which she won the Academy Award for Best Actress. This slim, blonde actress has also played against type, as a neurotic playwright in *The Royal Tenenbaums*.

Emma
(Miramax 1996)
ph: David Appleby

KEY FILMS
Hook, 1991
Seven, 1995
Emma, 1996
Sliding Doors, 1998
A Perfect Murder, 1998
Shakespeare in Love, 1998
The Talented Mr. Ripley,
 1999
The Royal Tenenbaums,
 2001
Shallow Hal, 2001
Possession, 2002

Shallow Hal
(20th Century Fox 2001)
ph: Glenn Watson

"The work gets more difficult as you get older. You learn more and you gather more experiences, there is deeper pain and higher highs."

The Talented Mr. Ripley
with Matt Damon
(Miramax/Paramount 1999)
ph: Phil Bray

Shakespeare in Love
with Joseph Fiennes
(Miramax/Universal 1998)
ph: Laurie Sparham

GREGORY PECK

Eldred Gregory Peck was born on April 15, 1916, in La Jolla, California. He attained major film stardom with his second movie, *The Keys of the Kingdom* (1944), and maintained that status for nearly fifty years. Whether in drama or romantic comedy, Peck's quiet strength and dignity always held him in good stead, making him one of the true movie greats. He was nominated four times for an Academy Award, and he won as Best Actor for his performance as the dedicated lawyer in *To Kill a Mockingbird*. Peck also received the Academy's Humanitarian Award in 1968 for his extensive charitable work. He died in 2003.

Studio Portrait
(1947)
ph: John Engstead

To Kill a Mockingbird
(Universal 1962)

KEY FILMS
The Keys of the Kingdom,
    1944
Spellbound, 1945
The Yearling, 1946
Duel in the Sun, 1946
Gentleman's Agreement,
    1947
Twelve O'Clock High, 1949
The Snows of Kilimanjaro,
    1952
Roman Holiday, 1953
Moby Dick, 1956
On the Beach, 1959
The Guns of Navarone, 1961
To Kill a Mockingbird, 1962
Cape Fear, 1962
The Omen, 1976
The Boys from Brazil, 1978

"*Gregory Peck is the hottest thing in town.*
Some say he is a second Gary Cooper. Actually,
he is the first Gregory Peck."

HEDDA HOPPER

Moby Dick
(Warner Brothers 1956)

Duel in the Sun
(Selznick/RKO 1946)
ph: Madison Lacy

Next page
Twelve O'Clock High
(20th Century Fox 1949)

MICHELLE PFEIFFER

The hauntingly beautiful Michelle Pfeiffer was born on April 29, 1958, in Santa Ana, California. A beauty-contest winner, she modeled before taking small parts in television and film. Featured roles in *Grease 2* and *Scarface* catapulted her to stardom. Pfeiffer has since demonstrated her considerable acting talent in both drama and romantic comedy, more than holding her own with such formidable leading men as Sean Connery *(The Russia House)* and Al Pacino *(Frankie and Johnny)*. Although she had previously sung in *Grease 2*, her sweet, sexy rendition of "Making Whoopee" in *The Fabulous Baker Boys* remains a memorable movie moment.

The Fabulous Baker Boys
(Gladden 1989)
ph: Karen Miller

The Age of Innocence
with Daniel Day-Lewis
(Columbia 1993)
ph: Phillip Caruso

KEY FILMS
Grease 2, 1982
Scarface, 1983
The Witches of Eastwick, 1987
Married to the Mob, 1988
The Fabulous Baker Boys, 1989
The Russia House, 1990
Frankie and Johnny, 1991
Batman Returns, 1992
Love Field 1992
The Age of Innocence, 1993
One Fine Day, 1996
What Lies Beneath, 2000

Love Field
(Orion 1992)
ph: Adger W. Cowans

Frankie and Johnny
with Al Pacino
(Paramount 1991)
ph: Andrew Cooper

"*She can do anything.*"

JONATHAN DEMME,
DIRECTOR

Dangerous Liaisons
with John Malkovich
(*Warner Brothers 1988*)
ph: Etienne George

Batman Returns
(WB/DC Comics 1992)
ph: Zade Rosenthal

BRAD PITT

William Bradley Pitt was born on December 18, 1963, in Shawnee, Oklahoma, and raised in Springfield, Missouri. Before finishing college he tried his luck in Hollywood and soon found work in television followed by small roles in films. Playing the sexy hitchhiker in *Thelma and Louise* put him on the path to major stardom and leading roles in films such as *A River Runs Through It*, *Seven*, and *Fight Club*. His image as a golden boy has placed him among the highest paid of Hollywood's younger stars. Determinedly choosing a wide variety of roles, Pitt was nominated for an Academy Award for his performance in *Twelve Monkeys*.

Interview with the Vampire
(Geffen 1994)
ph: Francois Duhamel

KEY FILMS
Thelma and Louise, 1991
A River Runs Through It, 1992
Interview with the Vampire, 1994
Legends of the Fall, 1994
Seven, 1995
Twelve Monkeys, 1995
Seven Years in Tibet, 1997
Fight Club, 1999
Spy Game, 2001
Ocean's Eleven, 2001

Seven
(New Line 1995)
ph: Peter Sorel

Ocean's Eleven
with George Clooney
(Warner Brothers 2001)
ph: Bob Marshak

Thelma and Louise
(MGM/Pathe 1991)
ph: Roland Neveu

"Success is a beast. And it actually puts the emphasis on the wrong thing. You get away with more instead of looking within."

Seven Years in Tibet
(Mandalay Ent. 1997)
ph: David Appleby

Fight Club
(20th Century Fox 1999)
ph: Merrick Morton

SIDNEY POITIER

Sidney Poitier was born in Miami on February 20, 1927, but spent all his early years as a citizen of the Bahamas, where he was raised. As an adult in New York, Poitier appeared on the stage before he landed his first film role. He made a strong impression in *No Way Out* and *Cry, the Beloved Country*, and his rise to stardom was swift. A talented actor and a charismatic screen presence, Poitier became the first black man to receive the Academy Award for Best Actor, given for his charming performance in *Lilies of the Field*. In 2002, in recognition of a highly distinguished screen career that has included directing and producing, the Academy presented him with an Honorary Award.

Guess Who's Coming to Dinner?
(Columbia 1967)

Buck and the Preacher
with Harry Belafonte
(Columbia 1971)

KEY FILMS
No Way Out, 1950
Cry, the Beloved Country, 1951
Blackboard Jungle, 1955
The Defiant Ones, 1958
Porgy and Bess, 1959
A Raisin in the Sun, 1961
Lilies of the Field, 1963
In the Heat of the Night, 1967
To Sir, with Love, 1967
Guess Who's Coming to Dinner? 1967
Uptown Saturday Night, 1974 (also directed)
Sneakers, 1992

No Way Out
with Mildred Joanne Smith
(*20th Century Fox 1950*)

The Defiant Ones
with Tony Curtis
(*United Artists 1958*)

In the Heat of the Night
(Mirisch/UA 1967)

Lilies of the Field
with Lilia Skala
(United Artists 1963)

"Here is a man who is dedicated to human rights and freedom."

DR. MARTIN LUTHER KING JR.

ELVIS PRESLEY

Elvis Aaron Presley, "The King," was born in Tupelo, Mississippi, on January 8, 1935, and spent his teenage years in Memphis. When he began singing professionally, merging rock and roll with the blues, his sweet, sexy voice, coupled with his swiveling hips, made him an instant teen sensation. From his first film, *Love Me Tender*, Presley displayed a charisma that matched

his stage and recorded performances. The public avidly followed his career, from his service in the Army, to his marriage and divorce, to his stage appearances in Las Vegas, to his tragic death in 1977. His thirty-three films, although not critically praised, always made money, and he sold over one billion record albums—more than any other singer in history.

Studio Portrait
(Paramount 1961)
ph: Bud Fraker

Love Me Tender
(20th Century Fox 1956)

KEY FILMS
Love Me Tender, 1956
Loving You, 1957
Jailhouse Rock, 1957
King Creole, 1958
Flaming Star, 1960
GI Blues, 1960
Wild in the Country, 1961
Follow that Dream, 1962
Roustabout, 1964
Viva Las Vegas, 1964

*"Take care of
the fans and
they will sure
as hell take
care of you."*

Jailhouse Rock
(MGM 1957)

Paradise Hawaiian Style
(Paramount 1965)

ROBERT REDFORD

Charles Robert Redford, born August 18, 1937, in Santa Maria, California, wanted to be a painter but drifted into acting. Stage and television appearances led to film parts and his breakthrough role in both the stage and film versions of the highly successful show *Barefoot in the Park*. Redford's good looks and intelligence have made him a top leading man, and his two films paired with Paul Newman, *Butch Cassidy and the Sundance Kid* and *The Sting*, proved box-office magic. Redford has directed six films, winning an Academy Award as Best Director for *Ordinary People*. He established the Sundance Institute in Utah, which gives a boost to aspiring filmmakers and is also active in environmental issues. He continues to act, his charismatic appeal undimmed.

Studio Portrait
(1966)

The Sting
(Universal 1973)

KEY FILMS
Barefoot in the Park, 1967
Butch Cassidy and the
    Sundance Kid, 1969
The Candidate, 1972
The Way We Were, 1973
The Sting, 1973
All the President's Men,
    1976
Brubaker, 1980
Out of Africa, 1985
Indecent Proposal, 1993
The Horse Whisperer, 1998
    (also directed)
Spy Game, 2001

The Electric Horseman
(Universal 1979)

Butch Cassidy and the Sundance Kid
with Paul Newman and Katharine Ross
(20th Century Fox 1969)

Indecent Proposal
with Demi Moore
(Paramount 1993)
ph: David James

The Way We Were
(Columbia 1973)

"Some people have analysis. I have Utah."

All the President's Men
with Dustin Hoffman
(Warner Brothers 1976)

KEANU REEVES

Born in Beirut, Lebanon, on September 2, 1964, Keanu Charles Reeves is a Canadian citizen with a Hawaiian name meaning "cool breeze over the mountains." As a teenager he began working on stage and television in Canada. He came to Hollywood's attention with *River's Edge* and played many teenage roles, including Ted in the highly successful *Bill & Ted's Excellent Adventure* and its sequel. It was his "growing up" in *Speed* that made him a big box-office draw. His good looks and enigmatic presence were shown to their best advantage in *The Matrix*, another enormous box-office success. Reeves continues to tour with his rock band, Dogstar.

Studio Portrait
(Warner Brothers 2001)
ph: Merie W. Wallace

Bill & Ted's Excellent Adventure
with Alex Winter
(Orion 1989)
ph: Phillip Caruso

KEY FILMS
River's Edge, 1986
Dangerous Liaisons, 1988
Bill & Ted's Excellent
   Adventure, 1989
Parenthood, 1990
Point Break, 1991
My Own Private Idaho, 1991
Much Ado about Nothing,
   1993
Speed, 1994
The Matrix, 1999
The Gift, 2000
The Matrix Reloaded, 2003

Speed
(20th Century Fox 1994)
ph: Richard Foreman

The Matrix
with Carrie-Anne Moss
(Warner Brothers 1999)
ph: Jasin Boland

"Keanu has an aloof quality, a far-away quality.
You can't quite get close to him, he is somehow unattainable.
That makes him very, very attractive . . ."

KENNETH BRANAGH,
DIRECTOR

BURT REYNOLDS

Burton Leon Reynolds Jr., born in Waycross, Georgia, on February 11, 1936, was a college football star until a knee injury made him rethink his future and he decided to pursue acting. After appearing on Broadway, Reynolds brought his macho, "good old boy" physicality to several successful TV series and then to the big screen, where his self-deprecating wit helped make him America's top box-office star in the 1970s. Although many of his films followed a formula of car stunts and antiestablishment comedy, Reynolds proved in *Deliverance* that he could excel in serious roles. He has tried his hand at directing and in recent years has been impressive in supporting roles. He was nominated for Best Supporting Actor by the Academy for *Boogie Nights*.

Boogie Nights
with Mark Wahlberg
(New Line 1997)
ph: Gillian Lefkowitz

KEY FILMS
Deliverance, 1972
The Longest Yard, 1974
Gator, 1976 (also directed)
Nickelodeon, 1976
Smokey and the Bandit, 1977
Semi-Tough, 1977
The End, 1978 (also directed)
Starting Over, 1979
City Heat, 1984
Switching Channels, 1988
Boogie Nights, 1997

Smokey and the Bandit
(Universal 1977)

"If you hold on to things long enough,
they get back into style . . . like me."

Deliverance
(Warner Brothers 1972)

JULIA ROBERTS

Julia Fiona Roberts was born in Smyrna, Georgia, on October 28, 1967. Following her older brother Eric into acting, she soon made her name with *Steel Magnolias*, receiving an Academy Award nomination as Best Supporting Actress. Her tall, lanky beauty and wide smile as well as her deft comic style powered the phenomenal box-office success of *Pretty Woman*. She capped her ten years of super-stardom with her Academy Award as Best Actress for *Erin Brockovich*.

Studio Portrait
(20th Century Fox 1991)

This performance combined her fine abilities as dramatic actress and light comedienne. Often termed "America's Sweetheart," Julia has been seriously involved in work for several UNICEF charities.

Erin Brockovich
(Universal 2000)
ph: Bob Marshak

KEY FILMS
Mystic Pizza, 1988
Steel Magnolias, 1989
Pretty Woman, 1990
Hook, 1991
Sleeping with the Enemy, 1991
The Pelican Brief, 1993
My Best Friend's Wedding, 1997
Runaway Bride, 1999
Notting Hill, 1999
Erin Brockovich, 2000
Ocean's Eleven, 2001

"You can be true to the character all you want,

but you've got to go home with yourself."

Pretty Woman
with Richard Gere
(Touchstone 1990)
ph: Ron Batzdorff

Steel Magnolias
(Tri-Star 1989)
ph: Zade Rosenthal

My Best Friend's Wedding
with Dermot Mulroney
(Tri-Star 1997)
ph: Suzanne Tenner

Sleeping with the Enemy
with Patrick Bergen
(20th Century Fox 1991)
ph: Myles Aronwitz

GINGER ROGERS

Virginia Katherine McMath, born on July 16, 1911, in Independence, Missouri, got her start as a dancer in vaudeville. Stage appearances on Broadway led to small film roles. Signed to an RKO contract, she was teamed with Fred Astaire, and in the ten films they made together they danced into movie history. The vivacious redhead proved herself a serious actress in *Kitty Foyle*, for which she won an Academy Award as Best Actress. Rogers excelled at romantic comedy and appeared opposite many of Hollywood's top leading men. When the movie parts ceased, she went back to Broadway and wrote her autobiography. She died in 1995.

Studio Portrait
(RKO 1936)
ph: Ernest Bachrach

The Barkleys of Broadway
with Fred Astaire
(MGM 1949)

KEY FILMS
42nd Street, 1933
Flying down to Rio, 1933
Roberta, 1935
Top Hat, 1935
Swing Time, 1936
Kitty Foyle, 1940
Roxie Hart, 1942
The Major and the Minor, 1942
The Barkleys of Broadway, 1949
Monkey Business, 1952

"It was tough being a woman in the theatrical business in those days."

Kitty Foyle
with James Craig
(RKO 1940)
ph: John Miehle

Once upon a Honeymoon
with Cary Grant
(RKO 1942)
ph: John Miehle

JANE RUSSELL

Ernestine Jane Geraldine Russell was born on June 21, 1921, in Bemidji, Minnesota. While studying acting, she was cast by Howard Hughes in his film *The Outlaw*. Hughes created an incredible advertising campaign for his film emphasizing the special cantilevered bra he had invented for the actress. Russell thus became a famous sex symbol before the film was even released. Her subsequent films showcased her versatility, and she held her own both against Robert Mitchum in the film noir *Macao* and as a wryly comic partner for Marilyn Monroe in *Gentlemen Prefer Blondes*. In the 1950s, Russell founded WAIF, a national adoption organization, for which she still works.

The Revolt of Mamie Stover
(20th Century Fox 1956)

Macao
with Robert Mitchum
(RKO 1952)

KEY FILMS
The Outlaw, 1943
The Paleface, 1948
His Kind of Woman, 1951
Macao, 1952
Gentlemen Prefer Blondes,
    1953
The French Line, 1954
Gentlemen Marry Brunettes,
    1955
Underwater! 1955
The Revolt of Mamie Stover,
    1956
Fate Is the Hunter, 1964

*"The girl with the summer-hot
lips . . . and the winter-cold heart."*

Publicity for *The Outlaw*

The Outlaw
(RKO 1943)
ph: George Hurrell

ARNOLD SCHWARZENEGGER

Arnold Alois Schwarzenegger was born on July 30, 1947, in Thal, Austria, the son of a police officer. He began his career as a bodybuilder, winning several titles including five as Mr. Universe, while studying for a degree at the University of Wisconsin. In the documentary film *Pumping Iron* he proved to be as charming as he was physically powerful, and the leading role in *Conan the Barbarian* turned him into an action superstar. His subsequent action films were huge money makers at the box office, but he also proved adept at comedy in *Twins,* with Danny DeVito, and as Emma Thompson's pregnant husband in *Junior.* Schwarzenegger became a U.S. citizen in 1983 and married the niece of President John F. Kennedy three years later.

Studio Portrait
(Columbia 1993)
ph: Zade Rosenthal

Terminator 2:
Judgment Day
(Carolco 1991)
ph: Zade Rosenthal

KEY FILMS
Pumping Iron, 1977
Conan the Barbarian, 1982
The Terminator, 1984
Commando, 1985
Predator, 1987
Twins, 1988
Total Recall, 1990
Terminator 2: Judgment
  Day, 1991
Junior, 1994

"I was always interested in proportion and perfection."

Kindergarten Cop
(Universal 1990)
ph: Bruce McBroom

Commando
(20th Century Fox 1985)

Twins
with Danny DeVito
(Universal 1988)
ph: Bruce McBroom

True Lies
(Universal 1994)
ph: Zade Rosenthal

FRANK SINATRA

Francis Albert Sinatra was born on December 12, 1915, in Hoboken, New Jersey. An early radio appearance led to work as a band singer, and by the early 1940s his captivating baritone had made him the idol of a generation of "bobby-soxers." He appeared in many musicals, including three classics co-starring Gene Kelly: *Anchors Aweigh*, *Take Me Out to the Ball Game*, and *On the Town*. In *From Here to Eternity* he proved his ability in dramatic roles, winning a Best Supporting Actor Academy Award. A turbulent romantic life and his "Rat Pack" antics created a "swinger" image that was reflected in his work in films, television, nightclubs, and the recording studio. His albums continue to be best-sellers, and his unique way of interpreting songs remains the template by which others are judged. Sinatra died in 1998.

Studio Portrait
(RKO 1951)
ph: Ernest Bachrach

From Here to Eternity
(Columbia 1953)

KEY FILMS
Anchors Aweigh, 1945
Take Me Out to the Ball
    Game, 1949
On the Town, 1949
From Here to Eternity, 1953
Young at Heart, 1954
Not as a Stranger, 1955
Guys and Dolls, 1955
The Man with the Golden
    Arm, 1955
High Society, 1956
Ocean's Eleven, 1960
The Manchurian Candidate,
    1962
Tony Rome, 1967

The Manchurian Candidate
with Laurence Harvey
(United Artists 1962)

On the Town
with Gene Kelly
(MGM 1949)

"Basically,
I'm for anything
that gets you
through the night—
be it prayer,
tranquilizers, or a
bottle of Jack
Daniels."

Ocean's Eleven
with Peter Lawford,
Dean Martin, and
Sammy Davis Jr.
(Warner Brothers 1960)

WILL SMITH

Willard Christopher Smith Jr. was born in Philadelphia on September 25, 1968. Working as a rap artist led to the leading role in the television series *The Fresh Prince of Bel Air*. During the series's six-year run, Smith's film roles in *Six Degrees of Separation* and *Bad Boys*, as well as his successful rap recordings, helped secure him the lead in *Independence Day*, which made him a major star. *Men in Black*, in which he forged an enjoyable comic partnership with Tommy Lee Jones, displayed his

engaging screen personality, but it was in the title role of *Ali*, for which he received an Academy Award nomination for Best Actor, that Smith proved his fine dramatic abilities.

Men in Black
(Columbia 1997)
ph: Andy Schwartz

KEY FILMS
Six Degrees of Separation, 1993
Bad Boys, 1995
Independence Day, 1996
Men in Black, 1997
Enemy of the State, 1998
The Legend of Bagger Vance, 2000
Ali, 2001
Men in Black II, 2002

Independence Day
with Jeff Goldblum
(20th Century Fox 1996)
ph: Claudette Barius

Ali
with Mario Van Peebles
(Columbia 2001)
ph: Frank Connor

KEVIN SPACEY

Kevin Spacey Fowler, born on July 26, 1959, in South Orange, New Jersey, grew up in southern California. He studied acting at the Julliard School in New York and gained stage experience while also working in comedy clubs where he excelled (and still does) at impersonations. Spacey has had a distinguished career in the theater, in both New York and London. He made an immediate impact in films, often playing "bad guys."

His Academy Award as Best Supporting Actor for *The Usual Suspects* resulted in major roles. Critics have raved about his subtle performances and his ability to shape the characters he plays with both humor and pathos. This was demonstrated to fine effect in *American Beauty*, for which Spacey won the Academy Award for Best Actor. He has formed his own production company to encourage new writers and directors.

Studio Portrait
(Icon 1999)
ph: Tom Collins

The Usual Suspects
(Gramercy 1995)
ph: Linda R. Chen

KEY FILMS
Glengarry Glen Ross, 1992
Swimming with Sharks, 1994
Seven, 1995
The Usual Suspects, 1995
Albino Alligator, 1996 (directed only)
Looking for Richard, 1996
L.A. Confidential, 1997
Midnight in the Garden of Good and Evil, 1997
American Beauty, 1999
The Shipping News, 2001

L.A. Confidential
(Monarchy/Regency 1997)
ph: Merrick Morton

American Beauty
(Dreamworks 1999)
ph: Lorey Sebastian

*"You always feel certain he's going to find
those moments that will make the hairs stand up on
the back of your neck."*

SAM MENDES, DIRECTOR

SYLVESTER STALLONE

Sylvester Enzo Stallone was born on July 6, 1946, in New York City, growing up there in the tough streets of Hell's Kitchen. After college he took various jobs while trying to work as an actor, eventually landing a featured part in *The Lords of Flatbush*. He then boldly created a vehicle for himself, writing and starring in *Rocky*, an enormously popular movie for which he was nominated as Best Actor. It won the Academy Award for Best Picture and spawned several sequels, all starring Stallone. He is also famous for his role as Rambo in the blockbuster series, and he proved himself a serious dramatic actor as the deaf police officer in *Cop Land*.

Studio Portrait
(United Artists 1982)

First Blood
(Carolco 1982)
ph: Joe Lederer

KEY FILMS
The Lords of Flatbush, 1974
Rocky, 1976 (also wrote)
Paradise Alley, 1978 (also
    wrote and directed)
Rocky II, 1979 (also wrote
    and directed)
Nighthawks, 1981
First Blood, 1982
Staying Alive, 1983 (directed
    only)
Rambo: First Blood Part II,
    1985
Cliffhanger, 1993
Cop Land, 1997

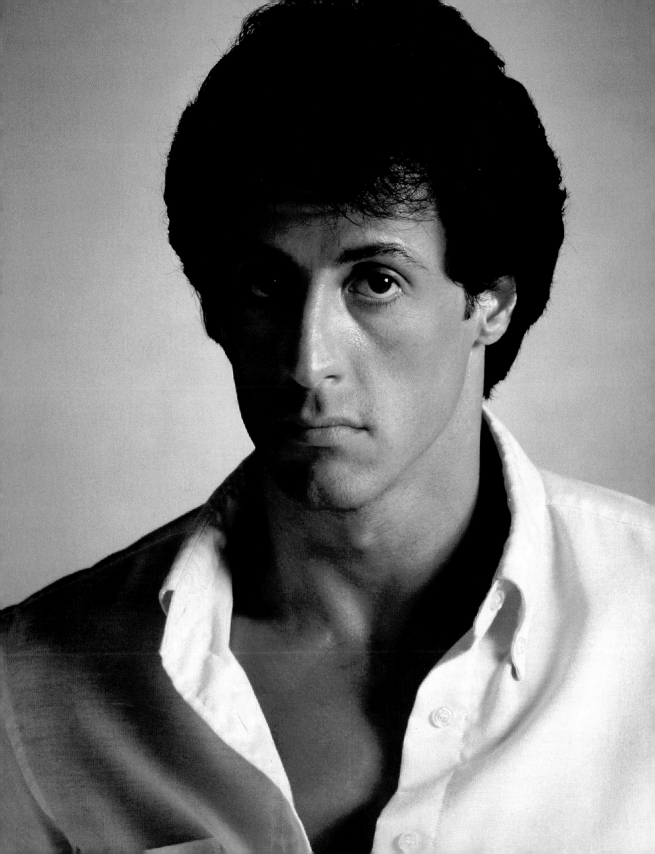

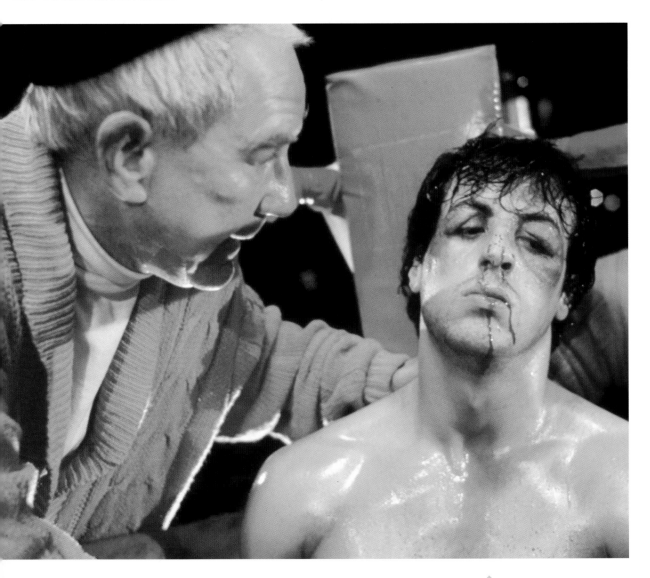

"The eyes droop, the mouth is crooked, the teeth aren't straight, the voice, I've been told, sounds like a mafioso pallbearer, but somehow it all works."

Rocky
with Burgess Meredith
(United Artists 1976)
ph: Elliot Marks

Cliffhanger
(Tri-Star 1993)
ph: Dirk Halstead

Daylight
(Universal 1996)
ph: Sam Emerson

Cop Land
(Miramax 1997)
ph: Sam Emerson

JAMES STEWART

James Maitland Stewart was born on May 20, 1908, in Indiana, Pennsylvania. A Princeton graduate, he acted on stage before making his first movie in 1935. Soon his shy, earnest screen persona was attracting audiences, and he capped his early career with an Academy Award for Best Actor in *The Philadelphia Story*. Stewart enlisted in the Air Force before Pearl Harbor was bombed, and he was awarded the Distinguished Flying Cross and the Croix de Guerre. In later years, he was promoted to Brigadier General in the Air Force,

Studio Portrait
(MGM 1938)
ph: George Hurrell

making him the highest ranking actor in military history. His postwar movies included several fine westerns and three films with director Alfred Hitchcock. He had four other Academy Award nominations and received the Academy's Honorary Award in 1985. By the time of his death in 1997, he was a revered American icon.

It's a Wonderful Life
(RKO 1946)
ph: Gaston Longet

KEY FILMS
Born to Dance, 1936
Mr. Smith Goes to
    Washington, 1939
Destry Rides Again, 1939
The Shop Around the
    Corner, 1939
The Philadelphia Story, 1940
It's a Wonderful Life, 1946
Winchester '73, 1950
Harvey, 1950
The Glenn Miller Story, 1953
Rear Window, 1954
Vertigo, 1958
Anatomy of a Murder, 1959
The Man Who Shot Liberty
    Valance, 1962
Flight of the Phoenix, 1966

**Mr. Smith Goes to
Washington**
with Jean Arthur
(Columbia 1939)

Vertigo
(Paramount 1958)

Winchester '73
(Universal 1950)

SHARON STONE

orn on March 10, 1958, in Meadville, Pennsylvania, Sharon Stone won the title of Miss Pennsylvania in a beauty pageant. She became a successful model, then began acting in minor film roles until she caught the public's attention in *Total Recall,* opposite Arnold Schwarzenegger. Her big break, playing

the seductive, bisexual writer in *Basic Instinct,* made her a bankable star. Stone, whose **IQ** is an impressive 154, won an Academy Award nomination for *Casino,* in which she played Robert de Niro's unhappy wife. She has formed her own production company and is also active as the spokesperson for **AMFAR,** the **AIDS** research foundation.

Basic Instinct
(Carolco 1992)
ph: Firooz Zahedi

KEY FILMS
Irreconcilable Differences, 1984
King Solomon's Mines, 1985
Total Recall, 1990
Basic Instinct, 1992
Sliver, 1993
Intersection, 1994
Casino, 1995
Sphere, 1998

Studio Portrait
(Morgan Creek 1996)
ph: James Bridges

Sliver
(Paramount 1993)

On fame: "It could walk into the room and eat you, or take you for a ride through a fabulous jungle—or it could slap the living daylights out of you, laugh, and leave."

Casino
(Universal 1995)
ph: Phillip Caruso

MERYL STREEP

Considered one of the foremost screen actresses of her generation, Mary Louise Streep was born on June 22, 1949, in Summit, New Jersey. After studying at the Yale Drama School, she worked on the New York stage. A small part in the film *Julia* (1977) launched Streep's career, which has seen outstanding performances in many distinguished films. *Kramer vs. Kramer* brought her an Academy Award for Best Supporting Actress, and she won the Best Actress award for *Sophie's Choice*. She has also had ten other Academy Award nominations. Although more frequently feted for her dramatic work, especially her mastery of many accents, Streep can also play comedy, and she astonished her admirers with her unexpectedly excellent singing voice in *Postcards from the Edge*.

Studio Portrait
(Columbia 1991)

Silkwood
(20th Century Fox 1985)
ph: Zade Rosenthal

KEY FILMS
The Deer Hunter, 1978
Kramer vs. Kramer, 1979
The French Lieutenant's Woman, 1981
Sophie's Choice, 1982
Silkwood, 1985
Out of Africa, 1985
Ironweed, 1987
A Cry in the Dark, 1988
Postcards from the Edge, 1990
The Bridges of Madison County, 1995
One True Thing, 1998
Music of the Heart, 1999
Adaptation, 2002
The Hours, 2002

Out of Africa
with Robert Redford
(Universal 1985)
ph: Frank Connor

Sophie's Choice
(Universal 1982)
ph: Josh Weiner

**The French
Lieutenant's Woman**
(United Artists 1981)
ph: Frank Connor

The Bridges of Madison County
with Clint Eastwood
(Amblin/Malpaso 1995)
ph: Ken Regan

"The oddest thing about being Famous with a capital F is that you're suddenly introduced to all these people you already know and they already know you. Except that you've never met them before."

ELIZABETH TAYLOR

Elizabeth Rosemond Taylor, one of the most beautiful female stars of all time, was born on February 27, 1932, in London to American parents who returned to the States in 1939. Strikingly beautiful even as a little girl, Elizabeth made her film debut in 1942 and was an important child star at MGM, capturing hearts in *National Velvet*. Growing up before the cameras, she made a seamless transition to major stardom. Academy Award nominations for her performances in *Raintree County*, *Cat on a Hot Tin Roof*, and *Suddenly Last Summer* featured less in the headlines than stories of her private life. Married eight times—twice to Richard Burton—Taylor won Academy Awards for Best Actress for both *Butterfield 8* and *Who's Afraid of Virginia Woolf?* In recent years she has accepted few acting roles, devoting much of her time to raising millions for AIDS research.

Cleopatra
with Richard Burton
(20th Century Fox 1963)

Studio Portrait
(Paramount 1954)
ph: Bud Fraker

KEY FILMS
National Velvet, 1944
Father of the Bride, 1950
A Place in the Sun, 1951
Giant, 1956
Raintree County, 1957
Cat on a Hot Tin Roof, 1958
Suddenly Last Summer,
   1959
Butterfield 8, 1960
Cleopatra, 1963
Who's Afraid of Virginia
   Woolf? 1966
The Taming of the Shrew,
   1967

National Velvet
with Mickey Rooney
(MGM 1944)

Suddenly Last Summer
(Columbia 1959)

**Who's Afraid of
Virginia Woolf?**
with Richard Burton
(Warner Brothers 1966)

Cat on a Hot Tin Roof
with Paul Newman
(MGM 1958)

*"There are three things
I never saw Elizabeth Taylor
do – tell a lie, be unkind
to anyone, or be on time."*

Mike Nichols

**The Taming of the
Shrew**
with Richard Burton
(Columbia 1967)

SPENCER TRACY

Spencer Bonaventure Tracy, considered by many the greatest movie actor ever, was born in Milwaukee, Wisconsin, on April 5, 1900. After serving in the Navy in World War I, he went to New York where he embarked on his acting career. Perhaps because he wasn't the typically handsome leading-man type, Tracy's movie career began slowly, and only after signing with MGM in 1935 was he given the meaty roles in which he effortlessly demonstrated his versatility. He won two Academy Awards as Best Actor, back to back, for *Captains Courageous* and *Boys Town* and received another seven Academy nominations throughout his distinguished career. One of the few actors to be loved and respected equally by audiences, critics, and his peers, Tracy had a long and successful partnership with Katharine Hepburn, both on and off screen, and they completed their ninth film together, *Guess Who's Coming to Dinner?* shortly before he died in 1967.

Studio Portrait
(MGM 1936)
ph: Ted Allan

Boys Town
with Mickey Rooney
(MGM 1938)

KEY FILMS
Fury, 1936
San Francisco, 1936
Captains Courageous, 1937
Boys Town, 1938
Woman of the Year, 1942
State of the Union, 1948
Adam's Rib, 1949
Father of the Bride, 1950
Pat and Mike, 1952
Bad Day at Black Rock, 1955
Inherit the Wind, 1960
Judgment at Nuremberg, 1961
Guess Who's Coming to Dinner? 1967

Father of the Bride
(MGM 1950)

The Sea of Grass
with Katharine Hepburn
(MGM 1946)
ph: C. S. Bull

"This mug of mine is as plain as a barn door. Why should people pay thirty-five cents to look at it?"

Bad Day at Black Rock
(MGM 1955)

JOHN TRAVOLTA

John Joseph Travolta was born in Englewood, New Jersey, on February 18, 1954. He dropped out of school to act and became a teenage heartthrob in the television series *Welcome Back, Kotter*. His third film, *Saturday Night Fever*, elevated him to stardom and brought him an Academy Award nomination. Critics once again praised his

Studio Portrait
(Universal 1978)
ph: Laurence L. Barbier

effortlessly sensuous dancing and charming good looks in the highly successful musical *Grease*. Throughout the 1980s, however, he suffered a slump in popularity. The success of Quentin Tarantino's *Pulp Fiction*, in which Travolta displayed unsuspected depths to his acting abilities, gave him a new audience, and suddenly Travolta was right back on top. He is now one of the highest paid and most sought-after stars in Hollywood.

Saturday Night Fever
with Karen Lynn Gorney
(Paramount 1977)

KEY FILMS
Carrie, 1976
Saturday Night Fever, 1977
Grease, 1978
Urban Cowboy, 1980
Blow Out, 1981
Look Who's Talking, 1989
Pulp Fiction, 1994
Get Shorty, 1995
Face/Off, 1997
Primary Colors, 1998
Swordfish, 2001

Grease
(Paramount 1978)
ph: Dave Friedman

"*Everything about my husband is
sexy, especially his lips.*"

KELLY PRESTON

Pulp Fiction
with Samuel L. Jackson
(*Miramax 1994*)
ph: Linda R. Chen

Get Shorty
(MGM 1995)
ph: Firooz Zahedi

LANA TURNER

Julia Jean Mildred Frances Turner, who was born in Wallace, Idaho, on February 8, 1920, grew up in California. Hollywood legend has it that, while a student at Hollywood High, Turner was discovered at a drugstore soda fountain. Signed by **MGM**, her first speaking part in *They Won't Forget* (1937) was a stepping-stone to stardom. Dubbed "The Sweater Girl" and turned into a blonde,

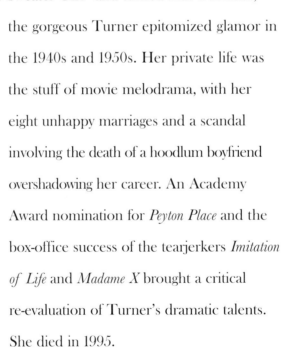

Studio Portrait
(MGM 1947)
ph: Eric Carpenter

the gorgeous Turner epitomized glamor in the 1940s and 1950s. Her private life was the stuff of movie melodrama, with her eight unhappy marriages and a scandal involving the death of a hoodlum boyfriend overshadowing her career. An Academy Award nomination for *Peyton Place* and the box-office success of the tearjerkers *Imitation of Life* and *Madame X* brought a critical re-evaluation of Turner's dramatic talents. She died in 1995.

The Postman Always Rings Twice
(MGM 1946)

KEY FILMS
Ziegfeld Girl, 1941
Honky Tonk, 1941
Johnny Eager, 1941
The Postman Always Rings
  Twice, 1946
Cass Timberlane, 1947
The Three Musketeers, 1948
The Bad and the Beautiful,
  1952
Peyton Place, 1957
Imitation of Life, 1959
Madame X, 1966

"I liked the boys and the boys liked me."

The Bad and the Beautiful
(MGM 1952)

Imitation of Life
with John Gavin
(Universal 1959)

DENZEL WASHINGTON

Denzel Washington, one of the finest actors of his generation, was born on December 28, 1954, in Mount Vernon, New York. After graduating from college he trained as an actor, making his name in the television series *St. Elsewhere*. In 1981, Washington made his film debut in *Carbon Copy*, but it was his powerful performance as the murdered antiapartheid leader Steve Biko in *Cry Freedom* that proved his potential, earning him an Academy Award nomination for Best Supporting Actor. Two years later he won the award for *Glory*. Washington's critically acclaimed leading performances have twice resulted in Academy Award nominations for Best Actor, and success came with his third, when he walked away with the statuette for *Training Day*.

Devil in a Blue Dress
(Tri-Star 1995)
ph: Firooz Zahedi

Glory
(Tri-Star 1989)
ph: Merrick Morton

KEY FILMS
Cry Freedom, 1987
Glory, 1989
Mo' Better Blues, 1990
Malcolm X, 1992
Much Ado About Nothing, 1993
The Pelican Brief, 1993
Philadelphia, 1993
Devil in a Blue Dress, 1995
The Hurricane, 1999
Training Day, 2001

*"I remain thankful for the gifts that
I've been given and I try to use them in a good way,
in a positive way."*

Malcolm X
with Delroy Lindo
(Warner Brothers 1992)
ph: David Lee

Training Day
(Warner Brothers 2001)
ph: Robert Zuckerman

JOHN WAYNE

John Wayne, throughout his career, epitomized for Americans the unbreakable spirit of their country. Born as Marion Robert Morrison, on May 26, 1907, in Winterset, Iowa, John Wayne grew up in southern California, working as a silent-movie extra during his college holidays. His genial, rugged, and honest demeanor brought him roles in at least seventy films, usually low-budget westerns, before *Stagecoach*, directed by John Ford, turned him into a star. During the following four decades, Wayne's image as an American patriot and hero complemented the classic films, directed by John Ford, in which he appeared. Late in his career he won an Academy Award as Best Actor for his warm and humorous portrait of an over-the-hill U.S. marshal in *True Grit*. "Duke" had made more than 250 pictures before he died of cancer in 1979.

Studio Portrait
(RKO 1957)
ph: Ernest Bachrach

The Searchers
with Jeffrey Hunter
(Warner Brothers 1956)

KEY FILMS
The Big Trail, 1930
Stagecoach, 1939
They Were Expendable,
  1945
Fort Apache, 1948
Red River, 1948
She Wore a Yellow Ribbon,
  1949
Sands of Iwo Jima, 1949
The Quiet Man, 1952
The Searchers, 1956
Rio Bravo, 1959
The Alamo, 1960 (also
  directed)
The Man Who Shot Liberty
  Valance, 1962
True Grit, 1969
The Shootist, 1976

The Spoilers
with Marlene Dietrich
(Universal 1942)
ph: Ray Jones

Stagecoach
(United Artists 1939)

Next page
Rio Grande
(Republic 1950)

"Talk low, talk slow, and don't say much."

The Quiet Man
with Maureen O'Hara
(Republic 1952)

Sands of Iwo Jima
(Republic 1949)

BRUCE WILLIS

Walter Bruce Willis was born on March 19, 1955, in Germany, but grew up in New Jersey. He worked as a bartender in New York while trying his luck at acting, getting occasional stage roles and bit parts in films. His breakthrough came with the popular television series *Moonlighting*, which made him a household name and won him an Emmy award. Leading film roles followed with *Die Hard* and its sequels, making him a top box-office star. This action hero also has proved to be a serious actor, most recently in *The Sixth Sense*, in which his fine, enigmatic performance successfully sustained the film's eerie atmosphere.

Studio Portrait
(Tri-Star 1991)
ph: Kerry Hayes

The Sixth Sense
with Haley Joel Osment
(Hollywood Pictures 1999)
ph: Ron Phillips

KEY FILMS
Blind Date, 1987
Die Hard, 1988
In Country, 1989
The Bonfire of the Vanities, 1990
Death Becomes Her, 1992
Pulp Fiction, 1994
Nobody's Fool, 1994
Twelve Monkeys, 1995
The Sixth Sense, 1999
Bandits, 2001

"Bruce is very powerful when he's still, when he's not blowing up half the known universe."

TERRY GILLIAM

Twelve Monkeys
(Polygram 1995)
ph: Phillip Caruso

Die Hard
(20th Century Fox 1988)
ph: Peter Sorel

NATALIE WOOD

Natasha Nikolaevna Zakharenko was born on July 20, 1938, in San Francisco, the daughter of Russian émigrés. She made her debut in films at eight and worked successfully as a child star, most memorably in *Miracle on 34th Street*. Easily making the transition to teenage parts and then adult leading roles, she collected three Academy Award nominations: *Rebel Without a Cause*, in which she played opposite screen icon James Dean; *Splendor in the Grass*, partnering with Warren Beatty in his first screen role; and *Love with the Proper Stranger*, opposite Steve McQueen. Extraordinarily

West Side Story
(Seven Arts/UA 1961)

beautiful, she played the lead in one of the most feted films of all time, *West Side Story*. She married and divorced actor Robert Wagner and was remarried to him at the time of her tragic death in a boating accident in 1981.

Studio Portrait
(Warner Brothers 1956)
ph: Bert Six

KEY FILMS
Miracle on 34th Street, 1947
Rebel Without a Cause, 1955
The Searchers, 1956
Splendor in the Grass, 1961
West Side Story, 1961
Gypsy, 1962
Love with the Proper Stranger, 1963
Inside Daisy Clover, 1966
This Property Is Condemned, 1966
Bob & Carol & Ted & Alice, 1969

"Natalie acts from her heart, not from the script."

ORSON WELLES

The Great Race
with Tony Curtis
(Warner Brothers 1965)

Gypsy
(Warner Brothers 1962)

THE KOBAL COLLECTION

The Kobal Collection owes its existence to the men and women of vision, courage, energy, talent, and beauty who created the movie industry and whose legacies live on through the films they have made, the movie studios and production companies they have built, and the photographs they have taken.

We collect, preserve, organize, and make these photographs available, and our success has helped to sustain and enhance the reputations of the actors, photographers, filmmakers, and studios and the films they created. We acknowledge their inestimable contribution and thank them for their continued support.

Page 2
Swing Time
Fred Astaire and
Ginger Rogers
(RKO 1936)

Pages 4–5
Rita Hayworth
(Columbia 1958)
ph: Bob Coburn

Pages 590–91
Funny Face
Audrey Hepburn and
Fred Astaire
(Paramount 1957)

Below
Camille
George Cukor directing
Greta Garbo and
Robert Taylor
(MGM 1937)
ph: Frank Grimes

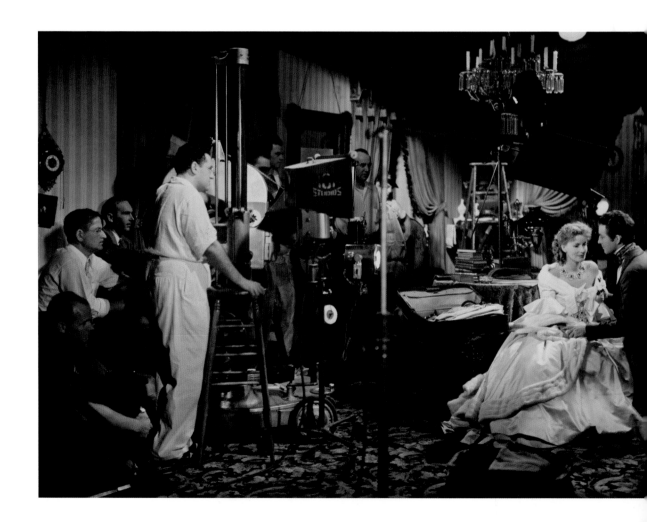